GRADE 2

e✓eryday Phonics
Intervention Activities

Table of Contents

Using Everyday Phonics Intervention Activities

Current research identifies phonemic awareness and phonics as the essential skills for reading success.

- **Phonemic awareness** is the ability to notice, think about, and work with the individual sounds in spoken words. Before children learn to read print, they need to become aware of how the sounds in words work. They must understand that words are made up of speech sounds, or phonemes.

- **Phonics** instruction teaches children the relationships between the letters (graphemes) of written language and the individual sounds (phonemes) of spoken language. Children learn to use the relationships to read and write words. Knowing the relationships will help children recognize familiar words accurately and automatically, and "decode" new words.

Although some students master these skills easily during regular classroom instruction, many others need additional re-teaching opportunities to master these essential skills. The Everyday Phonics Intervention Activities series provides easy-to-use, five-day intervention units for Grades K–5. These units are structured around a research-based Model-Guide-Practice-Apply approach. You can use these activities in a variety of intervention models, including Response to Intervention (RTI).

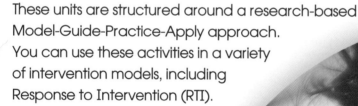

Getting Started

In just five simple steps, Everyday Phonics Intervention Activities provides everything you need to identify students' phonetic needs and to provide targeted intervention.

1. PRE-ASSESS to identify students' Phonemic Awareness and Phonics needs.

Use the pre-assessment on the CD-ROM to identify the skills your students need to master.

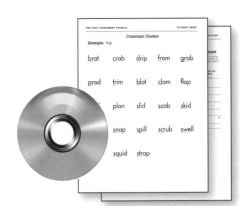

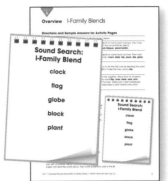

2. MODEL the skill.

Every five-day unit targets a specific phonetic element. On Day 1, use the teacher prompts and reproducible activity page to introduce and model the skill.

Day 1

3. GUIDE PRACTICE and APPLY.

Use the reproducible practice activities for Days 2, 3, and 4 to build students' understanding and skill-proficiency.

Day 2

Day 3

Day 4

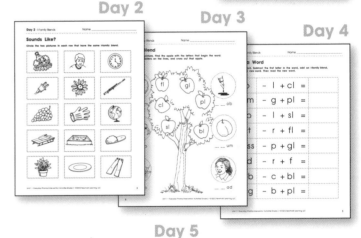

4. MONITOR progress.

Administer the Day 5 reproducible assessment to monitor each student's progress and to make instructional decisions.

Day 5

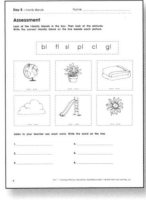

5. POST-ASSESS to document student progress.

Use the post-assessment on the CD-ROM to measure students' progress as a result of your interventions.

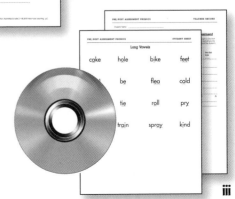

Standards-Based Phonemic Awareness & Phonics Skills in Everyday Intervention Activities

The Phonemic Awareness and Phonics skills found in the Everyday Intervention Activities series are introduced developmentally and spiral from one grade to the next. The chart below shows the skill areas addressed at each grade level in this series.

Everyday Phonics Intervention Activities Series Skills	K	1	2	3	4	5
Phonemic Awareness	✔	✔	✔	✔		
Letter Identification and Formation	✔	✔				
Sound/Symbol Relationships	✔	✔				
Short Vowels		✔				
Consonants		✔				
Long Vowels			✔	✔		
Blends			✔	✔		
Digraphs			✔	✔		
Variant Vowels			✔	✔		
CVCe Syllable Patterns			✔	✔	✔	✔
Closed Syllable Patterns				✔	✔	✔
Open Syllable Patterns				✔	✔	✔
r-Controlled Syllable Patterns				✔	✔	✔
Diphthongs				✔	✔	✔
Silent Letters				✔	✔	✔
Regular and Irregular Plurals				✔	✔	✔
Contractions					✔	✔
Prefixes					✔	✔
Compound Words					✔	✔
Comparatives						✔
Greek and Latin Roots						✔
Homographs and Homophones						✔
Word Origins						✔

Using Everyday Intervention for RTI

According to the National Center on Response to Intervention, RTI "integrates assessment and intervention within a multi-level prevention system to maximize student achievement and to reduce behavior problems." This model of instruction and assessment allows schools to identify at-risk students, monitor their progress, provide research-proven interventions, and "adjust the intensity and nature of those interventions depending on a student's responsiveness."

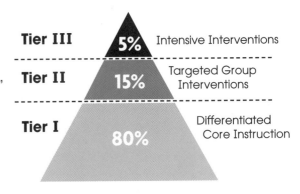

RTI models vary from district to district, but the most prevalent model is a three-tiered approach to instruction and assessment.

The Three Tiers of RTI	Using Everyday Intervention Activities
Tier I: Differentiated Core Instruction • Designed for all students • Preventive, proactive, standards-aligned instruction • Whole- and small-group differentiated instruction • Ninety-minute, daily core reading instruction in the five essential skill areas: phonics, phonemic awareness, comprehension, vocabulary, fluency	• Use whole-group comprehension mini-lessons to introduce and guide practice with comprehension strategies that all students need to learn. • Use any or all of the units in the order that supports your core instructional program.
Tier II: Targeted Group Interventions • For at-risk students • Provide thirty minutes of daily instruction beyond the ninety-minute Tier I core reading instruction • Instruction is conducted in small groups of three to five students with similar needs	• Select units based on your students' areas of need (the pre-assessment can help you identify these). • Use the units as week-long, small-group mini-lessons.
Tier III: Intensive Interventions • For high-risk students experiencing considerable difficulty in reading • Provide up to sixty minutes of additional intensive intervention each day in addition to the ninety-minute Tier I core reading instruction • More intense and explicit instruction • Instruction conducted individually or with smaller groups of one to three students with similar needs	• Select units based on your students' areas of need. • Use the units as one component of an intensive comprehension intervention program.

Overview   l-Family Blends

Directions and Sample Answers for Activity Pages

Day 1	See "Model l-Family Blends" below.
Day 2	Read aloud the title and directions. Invite students to name each picture. Then help students circle the two pictures that begin with the same l-family blend. (**clown/clock; flower/flute; glove/globe; sled/slipper; plant/plate**)
Day 3	Read aloud the title and directions. Invite students to name each picture. Then help students find and write the missing l-family blends. (**clam, blob, flip, plum, slip, glad**)
Day 4	Read aloud the title and directions. Model how to do the first one by reading the word **lip**. Then show how to take away **l** and add **cl** to make the new word **clip**.
Day 5	Read the directions aloud and name the pictures together. Allow time for students to complete the first task. Then pronounce the words **flip**, **clan**, **blob**, **sled**, **plot**, and **glum** and ask students to write them on the lines. Afterward, meet individually with students to discuss their results. Use their responses to plan further instruction and review.

Model l-Family Blends

◆ Hand out the Day 1 activity page and crayons.

◆ Write **pl-** on the board. Point to the letters as you **say:** *We play at a playground. When I say **play**, I blend **/p/** and **/l/** to make **/pl/**. This is an l-family blend.*

◆ Write **sl-**, **bl-**, **gl-**, **cl-**, and **fl-** on the board. Point to each blend in turn as you **say:** *People do other things at a playground, too. People slam dunk a basketball. They blow bubbles. They glide through the air on swings. They climb jungle gyms. They float on the pond in a rowboat.* **Slam**, **blow**, **glide**, **climb**, *and* **float** *all begin with l-family blends.*

◆ Ask students to look at the picture of the playground. **Say:** *Look at the flag. Say the word **flag** with me:* **flag**. *Listen as I say it again:* **/fl/ /a/ /g/**. *The **/f/** and **/l/** blend together to make **/fl/**.* **Flag** *begins with an l-family blend. Color the flag.*

◆ Repeat with **slide**, **flowers**, **plane**, and **cloud**. Then ask students to draw one more item that begins with an l-family blend. Invite them to share their drawings with the group.

◆ Point out objects you can see in the classroom that start with an l-family blend. Write a few on chart paper and read the words aloud. Then invite students to add to the list.

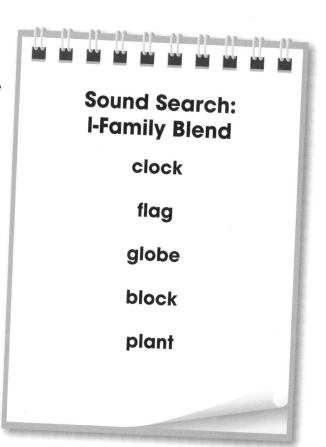

**Sound Search:
l-Family Blend**

clock

flag

globe

block

plant

Name _____

The Playground

Look at the picture. Color each thing that begins with an l-family blend.

Draw something else that begins with an l-family blend.

Sounds Like?

Circle the two pictures in each row that have the same l-family blend.

  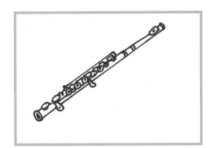

 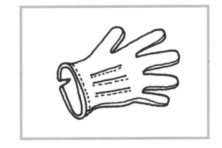 

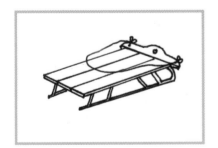 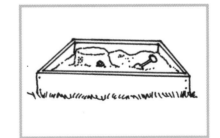 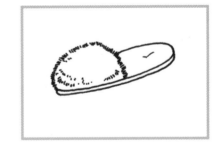

 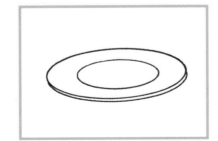 

Pick a Blend

Look at each picture. Find the apple with the letters that begin the word.
Write the two letters on the lines, and cross out that apple.

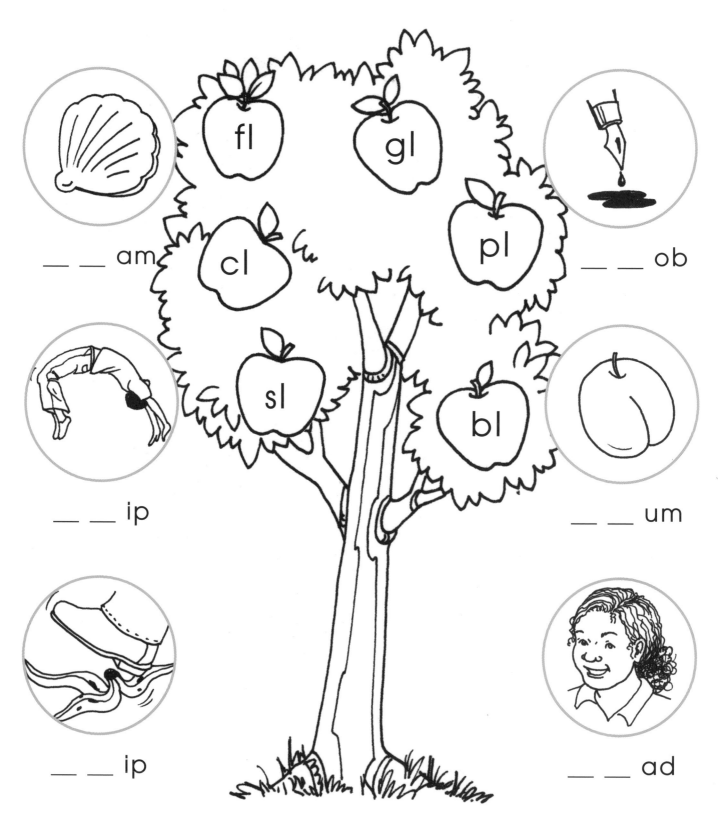

___ ___ am

___ ___ ob

___ ___ ip

___ ___ um

___ ___ ip

___ ___ ad

Name _____

Make a Word

Read the word. Subtract the first letter in the word, add an l-family blend, and make a new word. Then read the new word.

lip	– l + cl =	
gum	– g + pl =	
lap	– l + sl =	
rat	– r + fl =	
pass	– p + gl =	
cab	– c + bl =	
bug	– b + pl =	

Assessment

Look at the l-family blends in the box. Then look at the pictures. Write the correct l-family blend on the lines below each picture.

bl	fl	sl	pl	cl	gl

___ ___

___ ___

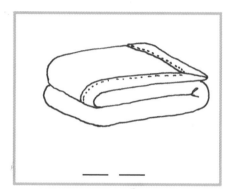
___ ___

___ ___

___ ___

___ ___

Listen to your teacher say each word. Write the words on the lines.

1. _____   4. _____

2. _____   5. _____

3. _____   6. _____

Overview   r-Family Blends

Directions and Sample Answers for Activity Pages

Day 1	See "Model r-Family Blends" below.
Day 2	Read aloud the title and directions. Invite students to name each picture. Then help students circle the two pictures that begin with the same **r-family** blend. (**brick/bridge; crayon/cry; drill/draw; truck/train; pretzel/present**)
Day 3	Read aloud the title and directions. Invite students to name each picture. Then help students find and write the missing **r-family** blends. (**crab, drip, frog, grin, press, trap**)
Day 4	Read aloud the title and directions. Model how to do the first one by reading the word **pan**. Then show how to take away **p** and add **br** to make the new word **bran**.
Day 5	Read the directions aloud and name the pictures together. Allow time for students to complete the first task. Then pronounce the words **brat**, **crop**, **drab**, **fret**, **grab**, **pray**, and **trip** and ask students to write them on the lines. Afterward, meet individually with students to discuss their results. Use their responses to plan further instruction and review.

Model r-Family Blends

◆ Hand out the Day 1 activity page and crayons.

◆ Write **cr-** on the board. Point to the letters as you **say:** *The princess wears a crown. When I say **crown**, I blend /k/ and /r/ to make /cr/. This is an **r**-family blend.*

◆ Write **fr-**, **pr-**, **gr-**, **br-**, **tr-**, and **dr-** on the board. Point to each blend in turn as you **say:** *What else happens in a palace? You might watch a frog turn into a prince or meet a greedy witch on a broomstick. Or perhaps you'll trap a dragon with great green eyes. The words **prince**, **frog**, **greedy**, **broom**, **trap**, **dragon**, **great**, and **green** all begin with **r**-family blends.*

◆ Ask students to look at the picture. **Say:** *Look at the dragon. Say the word **dragon** with me: dragon. Listen as I say it again: /dr/ /a/ /g/ /n/. The /d/ and /r/ blend together to make /dr/. **Dragon** begins with an **r**-family blend. Color the dragon.*

◆ Repeat with **broom**, **frog**, **grapes**, **trumpet**, and **princess**. Then ask students to draw one more item that begins with an **r**-family blend. Invite them to share their drawings with the group.

◆ Point out actions we do that begin with an **r**-family blend. Write a few on chart paper and read the words aloud. Then invite students to add to the list.

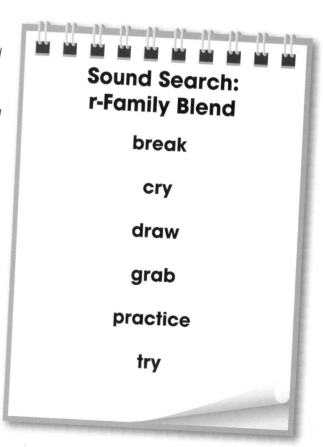

Sound Search: r-Family Blend

break

cry

draw

grab

practice

try

Name _____

The Pretty Palace

Look at the picture. Color each thing that begins with an r-family blend.

Draw something else that begins with an r-family blend.

Unit 2 • *Everyday Phonics Intervention Activities Grade 2* • ©2010 Newmark Learning, LLC

Sounds Like?

Circle the two pictures in each row that have the same r-family blend.

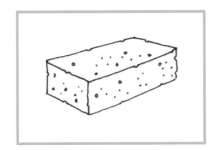  

 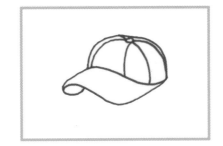 

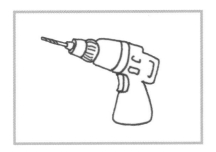  

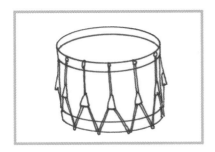  

Catch a Blend

Look at each picture. Find the fish with the letters that begins the word.
Write the two letters on the lines, and cross out that fish.

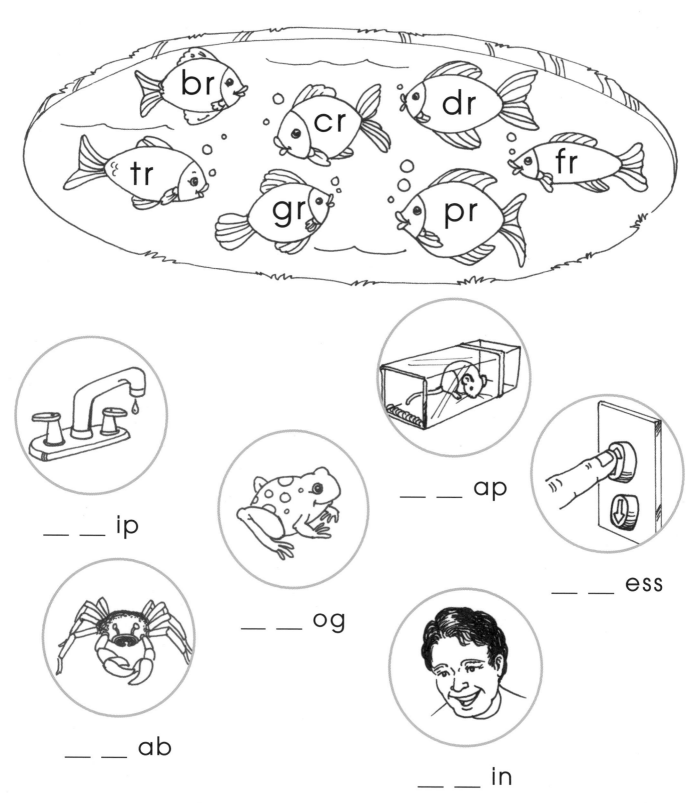

__ __ ip

__ __ og

__ __ ab

__ __ ap

__ __ ess

__ __ in

Make a Word

Read the word. Subtract the first letter in the word, add an r-family blend, and make a new word. Then read the new word.

pan	– p + br =	
fib	– f + cr =	
bag	– b + dr =	
pill	– p + fr =	
hip	– h + gr =	
mop	– m + pr =	
lot	– l + tr =	

Assessment

Look at the **r-family blends** in the box. Then look at the pictures. Write the correct r-family blend on the lines below each picture.

br	cr
dr	fr gr
pr	tr

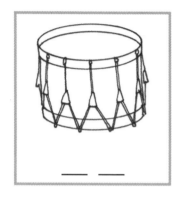
___ ___

___ ___

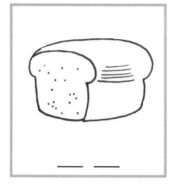
___ ___

___ ___

___ ___

___ ___

___ ___

Listen to your teacher say each word. Write the words on the lines.

1. _____

2. _____

3. _____

4. _____

5. _____

6. _____

7. _____

Unit 2 • Everyday Phonics Intervention Activities Grade 2 • ©2010 Newmark Learning, LLC

Overview   s-Family Blends

Directions and Sample Answers for Activity Pages

Day 1	See "Model Initial s-Family Blends" below.
Day 2	Read aloud the title and directions. Invite students to name each picture. Then help students draw a line between words with the same beginning **s**-family blend. (**snake/snore; sponge/spear; swan/swings; steak/star; scale/scooter**)
Day 3	Read aloud the title and directions. Invite students to name each picture clue, reminding them that each one begins with an **s**-family blend. Then help students complete the crossword by filling in the words. (Across: **1. sled**; **3. slip**; **4. stop**. Down: **1. swim**; **2. spot**; **3. snap**.)
Day 4	Read aloud the title and directions. Model how to do the first one by reading the word **tab**. Then show how to take away **t** and add **sc** to make the new word **scab**.
Day 5	Read the directions aloud and name the pictures together. Allow time for students to complete the first task. Then pronounce the words **scan, skin, slim, smug, snag, spur, stir**, and **swat** and ask students to write them on the lines. Afterward, meet individually with students to discuss their results. Use their responses to plan further instruction and review.

Model Initial s-Family Blends

◆ Hand out the Day 1 activity page and crayons.

◆ Write **sk-** on the board. Point to the letters as you **say:** *We skate around the rink. When I say **skate**, I blend /s/ and /k/ to make /sk/. This is an s-family blend.*

◆ Write **sl-, sp-, sc-, sm-, sw-, st-**, and **sn-**, on the board. Point to each blend in turn as you **say:** *There is lots of action at a skating rink. New skaters slip on the ice, which can make the sport a little scary. Most smile as they go round and round, building up a sweat. Skaters must stay warm or else . . . aah aah aah choo! They could sneeze on you!* **Slip, sport, scary, smile, sweat, stay**, and **sneeze** *all begin with* **s**-*family blends.*

◆ Ask students to look at the picture of the pond. **Say:** *Look at the snow. Say the word **snow** with me: **snow**. Listen as I say it again: /sn/ /o/. The /s/ and /n/ blend together to make /sn/. **Snow** begins with an **s**-family blend. Color the snow.*

◆ Repeat with **scarf, skate, spin, steam**, and **sweater**. Then ask students to draw one more item that begins with an **s**-family blend. Invite them to share their drawings with the group.

◆ Point out clothing that starts with an **s**-family blend. Write a few on chart paper and read the words aloud. Then invite students to add to the list.

**Sound Search:
s-Family Blend**

scarf

skirt

smock

sneakers

sports shirt

stocking

sweatshirt

Let's Skate

Look at the picture. Color everything that has an s-family blend.

Draw something else that has an s-family blend.

Match Up

Draw a line to match each pair of pictures that start with the same s-family blend.

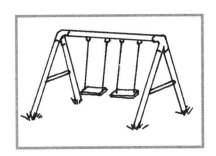

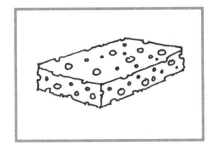

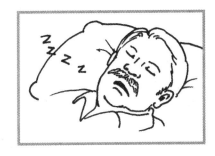

Crossword Puzzle

Say the name of each picture. Then write each picture name in the puzzle.

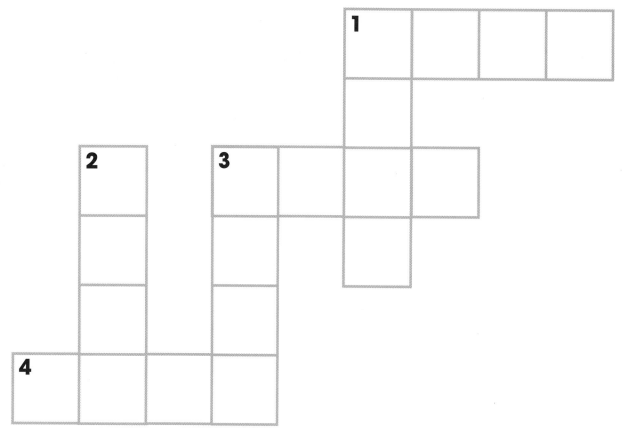

Across   ## Down

1    **1**

3    **2**

4    **3**

Make a Word

Read the word. Subtract the first letter in the word, add an s-family blend, and make a new word. Then read the new word.

tab	– t + sc =	
lid	– l + sk =	
fog	– f + sm =	
mob	– m + sn =	
kit	– k + sp =	
hem	– h + st =	
ram	– r + sw =	
cap	– c + sl =	

Assessment

Look at the s-family blends in the box. Then look at the pictures. Write the correct s-family blend on the line beside each picture.

sc sk sl sm sn sp st sw

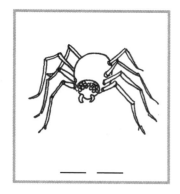 ___ ___

 ___ ___

 ___ ___

 ___ ___

 ___ ___

 ___ ___

 ___ ___

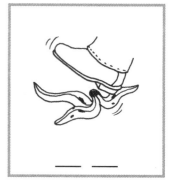 ___ ___

Listen to your teacher say each word. Write the words on the lines.

1. _____   5. _____

2. _____   6. _____

3. _____   7. _____

4. _____   8. _____

Overview Final s-Family Blends

Directions and Sample Answers for Activity Pages

Day 1	See "Model Final s-Family Blends" below.
Day 2	Read aloud the title and directions. Invite students to name each picture. Then help students glue the pictures that end with **/st/** under the ghost and the pictures that end with **/sk/** under the whisk. (Ghost: **vest**, **toast**. Desk: **mask**, **disk**.)
Day 3	Read aloud the title and directions. Invite students to name each picture, reminding them that each one ends with a final **s**-family blend. Then unscramble the word and write it on the line. (**test, desk, wasp, cast**)
Day 4	Read aloud the title and directions. Model how to do the first one by reading the word **mug**. Then show how to take away **g** and add **st** to the end to make the new word **must**.
Day 5	Read the directions aloud and name the pictures together. Allow time for students to complete the first task. Then pronounce the words **gasp**, **tusk**, and **pest** and ask students to write them on the lines. Afterward, meet individually with students to discuss their results. Use their responses to plan further instruction and review.

Model Final s-Family Blends

◆ Hand out the Day 1 activity page and crayons.

◆ Write **-st** on the board. Point to the letters as you **say:** *Camping is the best. When I say **best**, I blend /s/ and /t/ to make /st/. This is a final **s**-family blend.*

◆ Write **-st**, **-sk**, and **-sp** on the board. Point to each blend in turn as you **say:** *Our family likes to camp out. First, we hoist our tent on post. Then, at dusk, we make crisp smores. Camping is a blast!* ***First**, **hoist**, **dusk**, **crisp**, and **blast*** *all end with **s**-family blends.*

◆ Ask students to look at the picture of the family camping. **Say:** *Look at the kids as they roast the marshmallows. Say the word **roast** with me: **roast**. Listen as I say it again: /r/ /o/ /st/. The /s/ and /t/ blend together to make /st/. **Roast** ends with an **s**-family blend. Color the kids as they roast the marshmallows beside the fire.*

◆ Repeat with **nest** and **husk**. Then ask students to draw one more item that ends with an **s**-family blend. Invite them to share their drawings.

◆ Point out actions we do that end with an **s**-family blend. Write a few on chart paper and read the word aloud. Then invite students to add to the list.

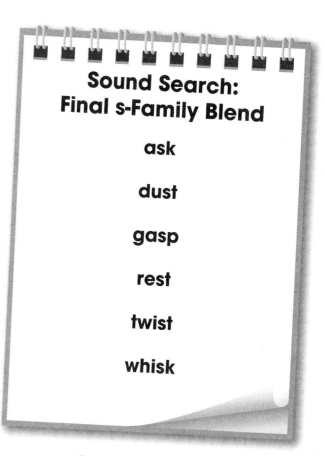

**Sound Search:
Final s-Family Blend**

ask

dust

gasp

rest

twist

whisk

Camp Out!

Look at the picture. Color everything that ends with an s-family blend.

Draw something else that ends with an s-family blend.

Match Up

Cut out the pictures. Glue the pictures with same ending sound as *ghost* next to the ghost. Glue the ones with the same ending sound as *desk* next to the desk.

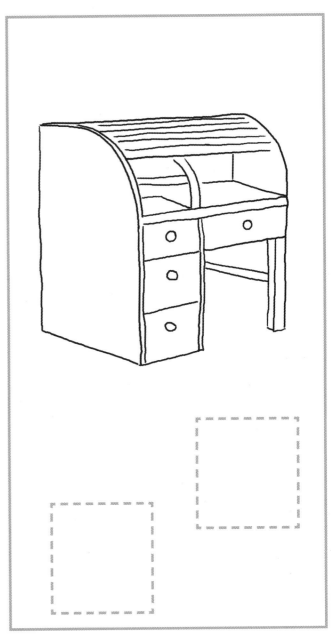

Word Mixer

These words are all mixed up! Say the name of the picture. Then unscramble the letters and write the words.

   s e t t → _____

   s d k e → _____

   w p s a → _____

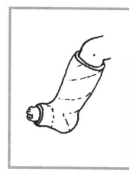   s c a t → _____

Name _____

Make a Word

Read the word. Subtract the last letter, add a final s-family blend, and make a new word. Then read the new word.

mug	– g + st =	
win	– n + sp =	
bar	– r + sk =	
lip	– p + st =	
cut	– t + sp =	
tan	– n + sk =	

Assessment

Look at the s-family blends in the box. Then look at the pictures. Write the correct s-family blend on the lines below each picture.

sk   sp   st

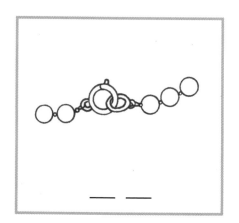

_____ _____

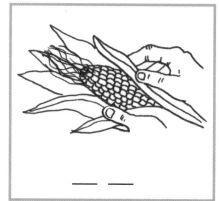

_____ _____

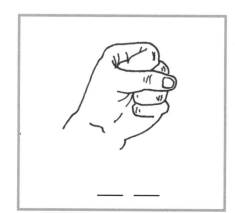

_____ _____

Listen to your teacher say each word. Write the words on the lines.

1. _____

2. _____

3. _____

Overview   Final Consonant Clusters

Directions and Sample Answers for Activity Pages

Day 1	See "Model Final Consonant Clusters" below.
Day 2	Read aloud the title and directions. Invite students to name each picture. Then help students circle the two pictures that end with the same final consonant cluster. (**king/swing; drink/skunk; wand/island; cent/paint**)
Day 3	Read aloud the title and directions. Invite students to name each picture. Then help students find and write the missing final consonant clusters. (**ring, wink, hand, tent**)
Day 4	Read aloud the title and directions. Model how to do the first one by reading the word **hid**. Then show how to take away **d** and add **nt** to make the new word **hint**.
Day 5	Read the directions aloud and name the pictures together. Allow time for students to complete the first task. Then pronounce the words **wing**, **junk**, **sand**, and **rent** and ask students to write them on the lines. Afterward, meet individually with students to discuss their results. Use their responses to plan further instruction and review.

Model Final Consonant Clusters

◆ Hand out the Day 1 activity page and crayons.

◆ Write **-nd** on the board. Point to the letters as you **say:** *We like the sound of a rock band. When I say* **sound**, *I blend /n/ and /d/ to make /nd/. This is a final consonant cluster.*

◆ Write **-nt, -ng, -nd,** and **-nk** on the board. Point to each blend in turn as you **say:** *People do other things at a concert, too. People chant and sing. They dance around. A concert cheers you up if you're in a funk!* **Chant, sing, around,** *and* **funk** *all end with a final consonant cluster.*

◆ Ask students to look at the picture. **Say:** *Look at the band. Say the word* **band** *with me:* **band**. *Listen as I say it again: /b/ /a/ /nd/. The /n/ and /d/ blend together to make /nd/.* **Band** *ends with a final consonant cluster. Color the leader of the band.*

◆ Repeat with **bang, chipmunk,** and **student**. Then ask students to draw one more item that ends with a final consonant cluster. Tell them it can be funny— something you might not see at a concert. Invite them to share their drawings with the group.

◆ Point out everyday things we do that end with a final consonant cluster. Write a few on chart paper and read the words aloud. Then invite students to add to the list.

**Sound Search:
Final Consonant Clusters**

paint

find

sing

drink

The Band

Look at the picture. Color the things that end with consonant clusters.

Draw something else that ends with a consonant cluster.

Sounds Like?

Circle the two pictures in each row that have the same final consonant cluster.

  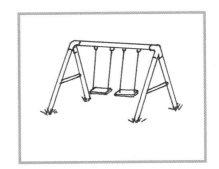

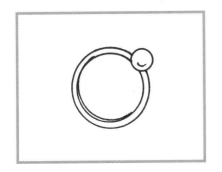 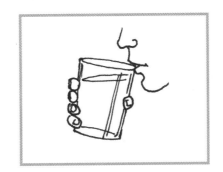 

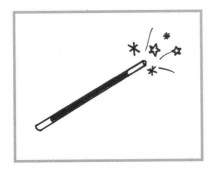  

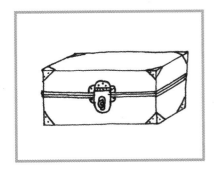  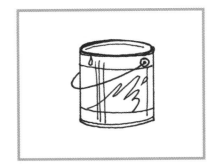

Cookie Jar

Look at each picture. Find the cookie with the final consonant cluster that ends each word. Write the two letters on the lines, and cross out that cookie.

ri __ __

te __ __

wi __ __

ha __ __

Make a Word

Read the word. Subtract the last letter in the word, add a final consonant cluster, and make a new word. Then read the new word.

hid	– d + nt =	
bet	– t + nd =	
pig	– g + nk =	
fat	– t + ng =	
hat	– t + ng =	
yam	– m + nk =	
let	– t + nd =	
web	– b + nt =	

Assessment

Look at the final consonant clusters in the box. Then look at the pictures. Write the correct final consonant cluster on the lines below each picture.

nd	ng	nk	nt

___ ___

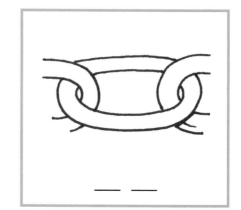

___ ___

___ ___

___ ___

Listen to your teacher say each word. Write the words on the lines.

1. _____

2. _____

3. _____

4. _____

Overview   Final Blends

Directions and Sample Answers for Activity Pages

Day 1	See "Model Final Blends" below.
Day 2	Read aloud the title and directions. Invite students to name the pictures in each row. Then help students circle the picture with the same final blend as the picture in the first column. (**stamp/lamp; scalp/gulp; belt/quilt; gift/lift**)
Day 3	Read aloud the title and directions. Invite students to read each sentence. Then help students circle the word with a final blend, and write the final blend on the line. (**lift, jump, gulp, melt**)
Day 4	Read aloud the title and directions. Model how to do the first one by reading the word **bun**. Then show how to take away the **n** and add **mp** to make the new word **bump**.
Day 5	Read aloud the directions and name the pictures together. Allow time for students to complete the first task. Then pronounce the words **pulp**, **damp**, **wilt**, and **loft** and ask students to write them on the lines. Afterward, meet individually with students to discuss their results. Use their responses to plan further instruction and review.

Model Final Blends

◆ Hand out the Day 1 activity page and crayons.

◆ Write **-lp** on the board. Point to the letters as you **say:** *We yelp with joy at the amusement park. When I say* **yelp**, *I blend /l/ and /p/ to make /lp/. This is a final blend.*

◆ Write **-lt**, **-ft**, **-mp**, **-lp**, and **-lt** on the board. Point to each blend in turn as you **say:** *Everyone loves an amusement park. Some rides tilt you from right to left. The roller coaster ramp carries you high into the air . . . take a big gulp . . . down you go until the ride finally comes to a halt.* **Tilt**, **left**, **ramp**, **gulp**, *and* **halt** *all end with final blends.*

◆ Ask students to look at the picture. **Say:** *Look at the raft. Say the word* **raft** *with me: raft. Listen as I say it again: /r/ /a/ /ft/. The /f/ and /t/ blend together to make /ft/.* **Raft** *ends with a final blend. Color the raft.*

◆ Repeat with **bump**, **melt**, and **help**. Then ask students to draw one more item that ends with a final blend. Invite them to share their drawings with the group.

◆ Point out actions we do that end with a final blend. Write a few on chart paper and read the words aloud. Then invite students to add to the list.

Sound Search: Final Blends

gulp

lift

jump

bolt

Name _____

The Fun Park

Look at the picture. Color the things that have final blends.

Draw something else that has a final blend.

Unit 6 • *Everyday Phonics Intervention Activities Grade 2* • ©2010 Newmark Learning, LLC

Name _____

Blend Match

In each row, find and circle the picture that has the same final blend as the picture on the left.

Final Blend Hunt

Find one word in each sentence with a final blend. Circle the word and write the final blend on the line.

He can lift a pig._____

Dad can jump._____

She can gulp._____

See it melt._____

Unit 6 • Everyday Phonics Intervention Activities Grade 2 • ©2010 Newmark Learning, LLC

Make a Word

Read the word. Subtract the last letter in the word and add a final blend to make a new word. Then read the new word.

bun	– n + mp =	
yet	– t + lp =	
win	– n + lt =	
rib	– b + ft =	
cat	– t + mp =	
kid	– d + lt =	
son	– n + ft =	

Assessment

Look at the final blends in the box. Then look at the pictures. Write the correct final blend on the lines below each picture.

ft	lp	lt	mp

— —

— —

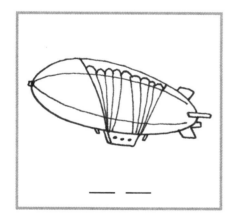

— —

— —

Listen to your teacher say each word. Write the words on the lines.

1. _____

2. _____

3. _____

4. _____

   Unit 6 · *Everyday Phonics Intervention Activities* Grade 2 · ©2010 Newmark Learning, LLC

Overview   Three-Letter Blends

Directions and Sample Answers for Activity Pages

Day 1	See "Model Three-Letter Blends" below.
Day 2	Read aloud the title and directions. Invite students to name each picture. Then help students draw a line between words with the same beginning three-letter blend. (**scroll/screwdriver; splint/splinter; strawberry/street; spring/sprinkles; squeeze/square**)
Day 3	Read aloud the title and directions. Invite students to name each picture. Then help students find and write the missing three-letter blends. (**scrub, strap, squat, spray, split**)
Day 4	Read aloud the title and directions. Model how to do the first one by reading the word **ham**. Then show how to take away **h** and add **scr** to make the new word **scram**.
Day 5	Read the directions aloud and name the pictures together. Allow time for students to complete the first task. Then pronounce the words **scrap, strum, sprig, splat**, and **squid** and ask students to write them on the lines. Afterward, meet individually with students to discuss their results. Use their responses to plan further instruction and review.

Model Three-Letter Blends

◆ Hand out the Day 1 activity page and crayons.

◆ Write **spl-** on the board. Point to the letters as you **say:** *We splash at the beach. When I say **splash**, I blend **/s/**, **/pl/**, and **/l/** to make **/spl/**. This is a three-letter blend.*

◆ Write **str-, scr-, squ-**, and **spr-** on the board. Point to each blend in turn as you **say:** *People do other things at the beach, too. Some people stroll along the shore. Children scream and squeal in the waves. And everyone sprays on suntan lotion. **Stroll, scream, squeal,** and **sprays** all begin with three-letter blends.*

◆ Ask students to look at the picture of the beach. **Say:** *Look at the straw. Say the word **straw** with me: **straw**. Listen as I say it again: **/str/ /aw/**. The **/s/**, **/t/**, and **/r/** blend together to make **/str/**. **Straw** begins with a three-letter blend. Color the straw.*

◆ Repeat with **splash, spray, square**, and **scratch**. Then ask students to draw one more item that begins with a three-letter blend. Invite them to share their drawings with the group.

◆ Point out actions we do that begin with a three-letter blend. Write a few on chart paper and read the words aloud. Then invite students to add to the list.

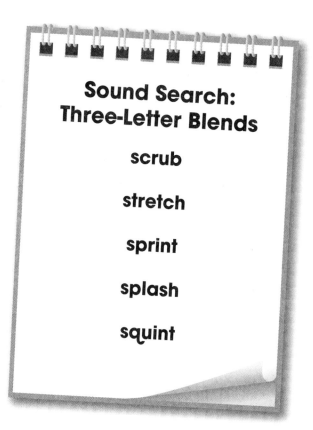

Sound Search: Three-Letter Blends

scrub

stretch

sprint

splash

squint

Beach Day

Look at the picture. Color the things that have a three-letter blend.

Draw something else that has a three-letter blend.

Match Up

Draw a line to match each pair of pictures that starts with the same three-letter blend.

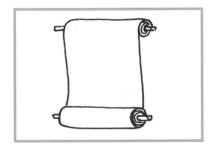

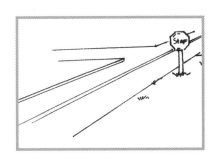

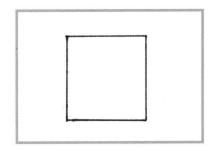

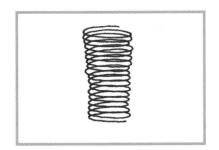

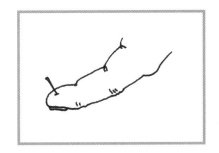

Scoop a Blend

Look at each picture. Find the ice cream cone with the three-letter blend that begins the word. Write the letters on the lines, and cross out the cone.

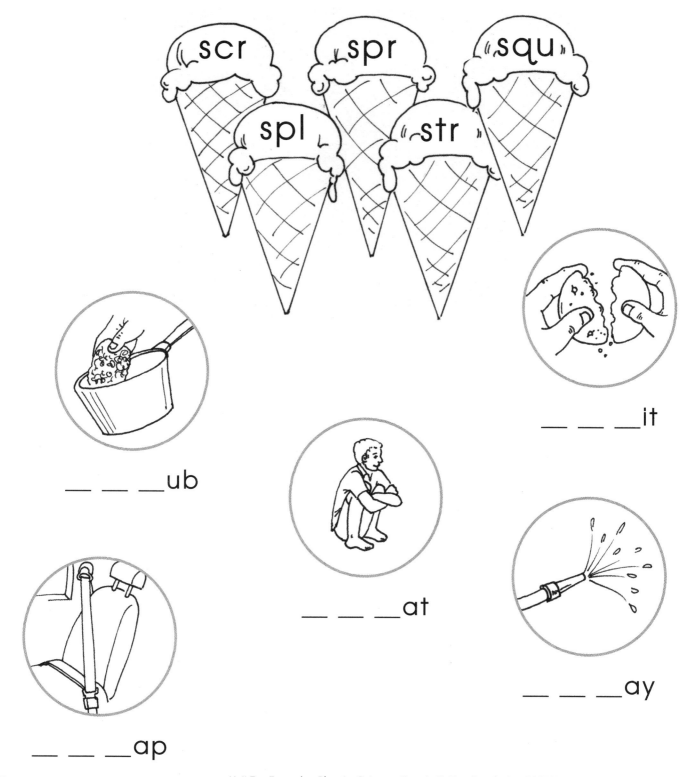

scr spr squ spl str

__ __ __ub

__ __ __it

__ __ __at

__ __ __ay

__ __ __ap

Make a Word

Read the word. Subtract the first letter in the word, add a three-letter blend, and make a new word. Then read the new word.

ham	–h + scr =	
cut	–c + str =	
bang	–b + spr =	
mint	–m + spl =	
lint	–l + squ=	

Assessment

Look at the three-letter blends in the box. Then look at the pictures. Write the correct three-letter blend on the lines below each picture.

scr spl spr str squ

__ __ __

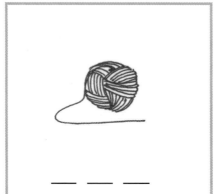

__ __ __

__ __ __

__ __ __

__ __ __

Listen to your teacher say each word. Write the words on the lines.

1. _____   4. _____

2. _____   5. _____

3. _____

Overview   CVCe (Long a)

Directions and Sample Answers for Activity Pages

Day 1	See "Model CVCe Long a" below.
Day 2	Read aloud the title and directions. Invite students to name the pictures in each row. Then help students circle the picture with a long **a** sound. (**snake, plane, grapes, plate, cave**)
Day 3	Read aloud the title and directions. Invite students to name each picture clue. Tell them that each word has a long **a** sound and a vowel/consonant/final **e** pattern. Then help students complete the crossword. (Across: **3. rake; 6. cane; 7. vase.** Down: **1. maze; 2. gate; 4. tape; 5. wave.**)
Day 4	Read aloud the title and directions. Model how to do the first one by reading the word **hat**. Point out the short **a** sound. Then show how to add final **e** to make the new word **hate**. Point out how the consonant/vowel/final **e** creates a long **a** sound.
Day 5	Read the directions aloud and name the pictures together. Allow time for students to complete the first task. Then pronounce the words **jade, take, pale, name, sane, nape, case, rate**, and **gaze** and ask students to write them on the lines. Afterward, meet individually with students to discuss their results. Use their responses to plan further instruction and review.

Model CVCe Long a

◆ Hand out the Day 1 activity page and crayons.

◆ **Say:** *Jane likes to bake. Listen for the middle sound as I say the word **bake** slowly: **/b/ / ā/ /k/**. The middle sound in **bake** is the long **a** sound, or **/ā/**.*

◆ Write **bake** on the board. **Say:** *In **bake**, a consonant and final **e** follow the vowel. When you see **a** followed by a consonant and final **e**, it usually stands for a long **a** sound. Point to the letters as you blend the sounds again: **/b/ / ā / /k/**.*

◆ Ask students to look at the picture. Write **Jane** on the board. **Say:** *Look at the name **Jane**. Say **Jane** with me: **Jane**. Listen as I say it slowly: **/j/ /ā / /n/**. **Jane** has a long **a** sound because **a** is followed by a consonant and final **e**. Color in Jane.*

◆ Help students find and color the other pictures that have the long **a** sound. Write the words on the board as you find them, including **cake, flame,** and **vase**. Read each word slowly, pointing out the vowel/consonant/final **e** pattern.

◆ Point out objects you can see in the classroom that have a long **a** sound. Write a few on chart paper and read the words aloud. Then invite students to add to the list.

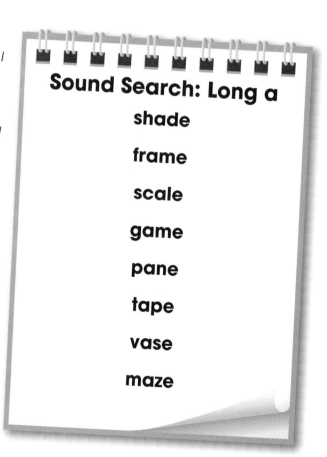

Sound Search: Long a

shade

frame

scale

game

pane

tape

vase

maze

Jane Bakes a Cake

Look at the picture. Color the things that have a long *a* sound.

Sounds Like?

Circle the picture in each row that has the long *a* sound you hear in *name*.

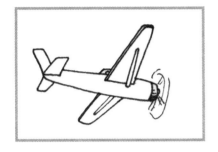  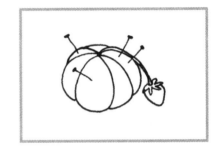

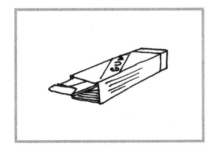 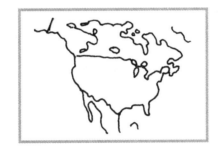 

 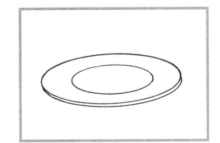 

Crossword Puzzle

Say the name of each picture. Then write each picture name in the puzzle.

Across

3

6

7

Down

1

4

2

5

Short a to Long a

Read the word. Add final *e* to make a new word with a long *a* sound. Then read the new word.

hat	+ e =	
fad	+ e =	
pal	+ e =	
pan	+ e =	
bad	+ e =	
cap	+ e =	
fat	+ e =	
rat	+ e =	

Assessment

Look at the picture pairs. Circle the one with the long *a* sound. Then write the missing letters for both picture words on the lines.

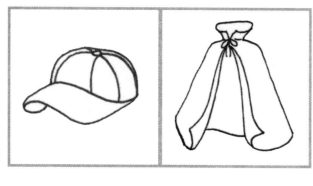

ca __   ca __ __

va __ __   va __

ma __   ma __ __

Listen to your teacher say each word. Write the words on the lines.

1. _____

2. _____

3. _____

4. _____

5. _____

6. _____

7. _____

8. _____

9. _____

    Unit 8 • *Everyday Phonics Intervention Activities Grade 2* • ©2010 Newmark Learning, LLC

Overview   CVCe (Long o)

Directions and Sample Answers for Activity Pages

Day 1	See "Model CVCe Long o" below.
Day 2	Read aloud the title and directions. Invite students to name the pictures. Then help students color the pictures with a long **o** sound blue and pictures with the short **o** sound red. (Blue: **globe**, **rope**, **nose**, **stove**, **phone**. Red: **pot**, **sock**, **fox**, **mop**, **frog**.)
Day 3	Read aloud the title and directions. Invite students to name each picture. Then help students find and write the missing vowel/consonant/final **e** pattern. (**bone, pole, robe, poke, stove, home**)
Day 4	Read aloud the title and directions. Model how to do the first one by reading the word **rod**. Point out the short **o** sound. Then show how to add final **e** to make the new word **rode**. Point out how the consonant/vowel/final **e** creates a long **o** sound.
Day 5	Read the directions and the words aloud together. Allow time for students to complete the first task. Then pronounce the words **lobe**, **code**, **joke**, **mole**, **Nome**, **zone**, **cope**, **rote**, and **wove** and ask students to write them on the lines. Afterward, meet individually with students to discuss their results. Use their responses to plan further instruction and review.

Model CVCe Long o

◆ Hand out the Day 1 activity page and crayons.

◆ **Say:** *We have a garden at our home. Listen for the middle sound as I say the word home slowly: /h/ /ō/ /m/. The middle sound in home is the long o sound, or /ō/.*

◆ Write **home** on the board. **Say:** *In home, a consonant and final e follow the vowel. When you see o followed by a consonant and final e, it usually stands for a long o sound.* Point to the letters as you blend the sounds again: **/h/ /ō/ /m/**.

◆ Ask students to look at the picture. Write **hole** on the board. **Say:** *Look at the word hole. Say hole with me: hole. Listen as I say it slowly: /h/ /ō/ /l/. Hole has a long o sound because o is followed by a consonant and final e. Color in the hole.*

◆ Help students find and color the other pictures that have the long **o** sound. Write the words on the board as you find them, including **hose**, **rose**, **stone**, and **mole**. Read each word slowly, pointing out the vowel/consonant/final **e** pattern.

◆ Say aloud some things we do that have a long **o** sound in them. Write a few on chart paper and read the words aloud. Then invite students to add to the list.

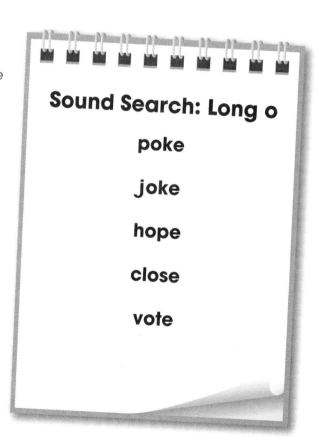

Sound Search: Long o

poke

joke

hope

close

vote

Our Garden

Look at the picture. Color the things that have a long *o* sound.

Long o or Short o?

Color the pictures with the long *o* sound, as in *hope*, blue. Color the pictures with short *o* sound, as in *hot*, red.

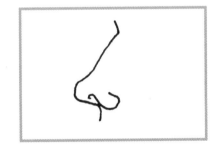

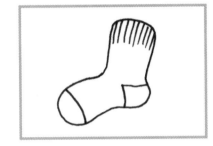

Note It!

Look at each picture. Find the sticky note with the vowel/consonant/final *e* pattern that completes the word. Write the letters on the lines, and cross out the sticky note.

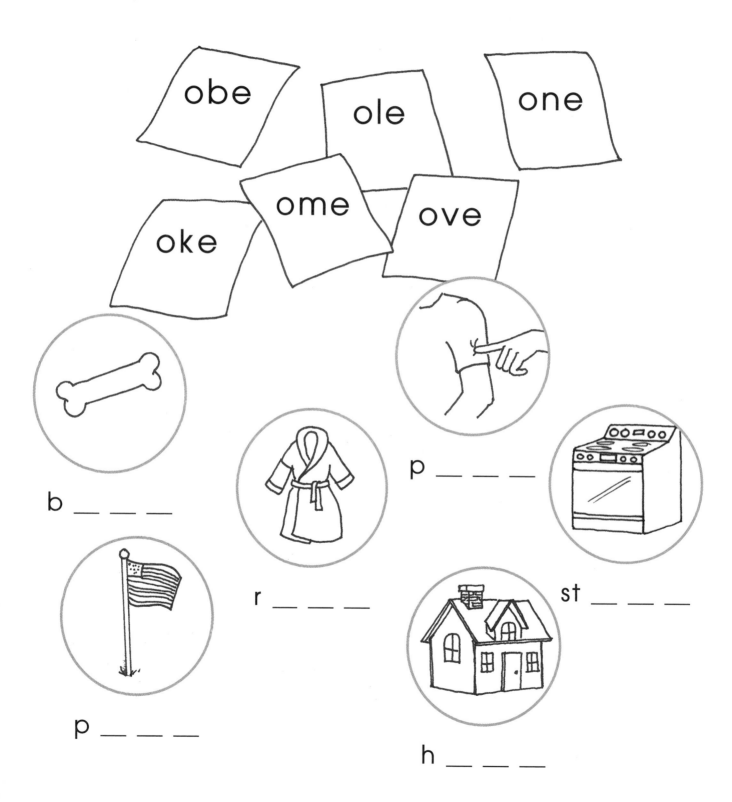

obe

ole

one

ome

ove

oke

b _ _ _

r _ _ _

p _ _ _

p _ _ _

st _ _ _

h _ _ _

Short o to Long o

Read the word. Add final *e* to make a new word with a long *o* sound. Then read the new word.

rod	+ e =	
not	+ e =	
lob	+ e =	
con	+ e =	
hop	+ e =	
slop	+ e =	
dot	+ e =	

Name _____

Assessment

Read the words. Circle the ones that have the long *o* sound.

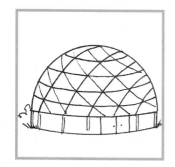   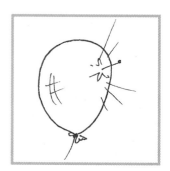

Listen to your teacher say each word. Write the words on the lines.

1. _____

2. _____

3. _____

4. _____

5. _____

6. _____

7. _____

8. _____

9. _____

 Unit 9 • Everyday Phonics Intervention Activities Grade 2 • ©2010 Newmark Learning, LLC

Overview   CVCe (Long i)

Directions and Sample Answers for Activity Pages

Day 1	See "Model CVCe Long i" below.
Day 2	Read aloud the title and directions. Invite students to name the pictures in each row. Then help students circle the pictures with a long **i** sound. (**price, knife, bride, smile, write, drive**)
Day 3	Read aloud the title and directions. Invite students to name each picture clue. Tell them that each word has a long **i** sound and a vowel/consonant/final **e** pattern. Then help students complete the crossword. (Across: **2. line**; **4. bike**; **6. slide**; **7. pipe**. Down: **1. kite**; **3. lime**; **7. hive**.)
Day 4	Read aloud the title and directions. Model how to do the first one by reading the word **fin**. Point out the short **i** sound. Then show how to add final **e** to make the new word **fine**. Point out how the consonant/vowel/final **e** creates a long **i** sound.
Day 5	Read the directions and the words aloud. Allow time for students to complete the first task. Then pronounce the words **tide**, **life**, **like**, **time**, **fine**, **wipe**, **kite**, and **jive** and ask students to write them on the lines. Afterward, meet individually with students to discuss their results. Use their responses to plan further instruction and review.

Model CVCe Long i

Sound Search: Long i

hide

bike

smile

dine

dive

◆ Hand out the Day 1 activity page and crayons.

◆ **Say:** *We like to hike. Listen for the middle sound as I say the word* **hike** *slowly:* **/h/ /ī/ /k/**. *The middle sound in* **hike** *is the long* **i** *sound, or* **/ī/**.

◆ Write **hike** on the board. **Say:** *In* **hike**, *a consonant and final* **e** *follow the vowel. When you see* **i** *followed by a consonant and final* **e**, *it usually stands for a long* **i** *sound.* Point to the letters as you blend the sounds again: **/h/ /ī/ /k/**.

◆ Ask students to look at the picture. Look at the bug bite on the girl's arm. Write **bite** on the board. **Say:** *Look at the word* **bite**. *Say* **bite** *with me:* **bite**. *Listen as I say it slowly:* **/b/ /ī/ /t/**. **Bite** *has a long* **i** *sound because* **i** *is followed by a consonant and final* **e**. *Color in the bite.*

◆ Help students find and color the other pictures that have the long **i** sound. Write the words on the board as you find them, including **vine**, **mice**, **wipe**, and **five**. Read each word slowly, pointing out the vowel/consonant/final **e** pattern.

◆ Point out actions we do that have a long **i** sound in them. Write a few on chart paper and read the words aloud. Then invite students to add to the list.

We Like to Hike

Look at the picture. Color the things that have a long *i* sound.

Sounds Like?

Circle the picture in each row that has the long *i* sound you hear in *like*.

Crossword Puzzle

Say the name of each picture. Then write each picture name in the puzzle.

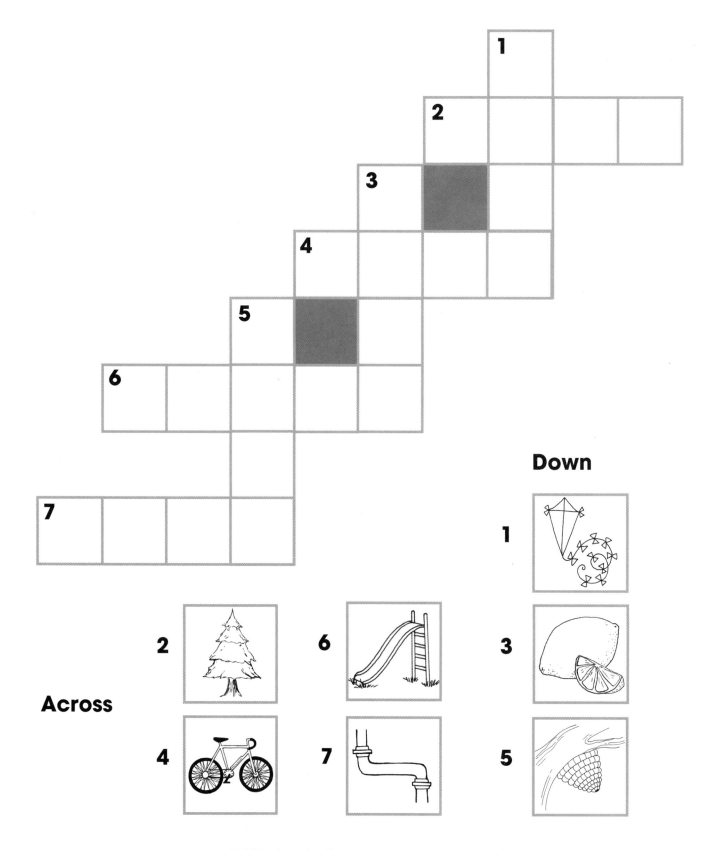

Down

Across

Short i to Long i

Read the word. Add final *e* to make a new word with a long *i* sound. Then read the new word.

fin	+ e =	
hid	+ e =	
dim	+ e =	
rip	+ e =	
spin	+ e =	
rid	+ e =	
slim	+ e =	
strip	+ e =	

Assessment

Read the words. Circle the ones that have the long *i* sound.

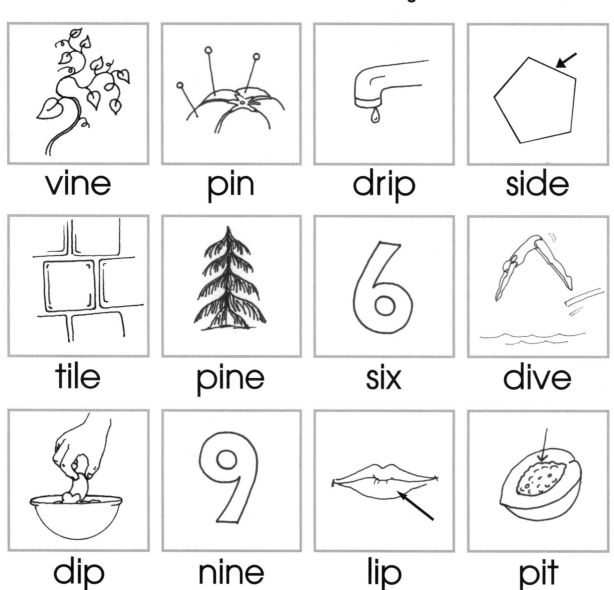

vine   pin   drip   side

tile   pine   six   dive

dip   nine   lip   pit

Listen to your teacher say each word. Write the words on the lines.

1. _____

2. _____

3. _____

4. _____

5. _____

6. _____

7. _____

8. _____

Overview   Open Vowels

Directions and Sample Answers for Activity Pages

Day 1	See "Model Open Vowels" below.
Day 2	Read aloud the title and directions. Have students read the words. Then help them glue the words that end with **/ē/** under the tree, and the ones that end with **/ō/** under the rhino. (Tree: **he**, **be**, **we**, **me**. Rhino: **go**, **so**, **no**, **Jo**.)
Day 3	Read aloud the title and directions. Invite students to read each sentence. Then help students circle the word and write the open vowel. (**see, go, we, he, no**)
Day 4	Read aloud the title and directions. Model how to do the first one by reading the word **got**. Point out the short **o** sound. Then show how to subtract the consonant to make the new word **go**. Point out how the open vowel creates a long **o** sound.
Day 5	Read the directions aloud and name the pictures together. Allow time for students to complete the first task. Then pronounce the words **be**, **he**, **me**, **we**, **go**, **no**, and **so** and ask students to write them on the lines. Afterward, meet individually with students to discuss their results. Use their responses to plan further instruction and review.

Model Open Vowels

◆ Hand out the Day 1 activity page and crayons.

◆ **Say:** *Look at me! Listen for the ending sound as I say the word **me** again: /mē/. The word **me** has the long **e** vowel sound at the end. Listen again to the ending sound: /mē/.*

◆ Write **go** on the board. **Say:** *The word **go** ends with a long vowel sound, too. It ends with the long **o** sound, or /ō/. Listen again as I blend the sounds /g/ /ō/.* Explain that when a vowel doesn't have another letter after it, it is called an open vowel and it stands for the long vowel sound.

◆ Ask students to look at the first picture on the activity page. Write **no** on the board. **Say:** *Look at the word **no**. Say **no** with me: **no**. The **o** in **no** is an open vowel, and so it has a long **o** sound. Let's listen to the last sound again: /nō/. I hear /ō/. Write **o** on the line.*

◆ Help students identify the ending vowel sound—either /ō/ or /ē/—in the rest of the pictures. Write the words on the board if necessary: **yo-yo**, **tomato**, **tree**, **radio**, **piano**, **zero**, **bee**, and **knee**. Read each word slowly, pointing out the open vowel.

◆ Point out names of characters or real people that have an open vowel. Write a few on chart paper and read them aloud.

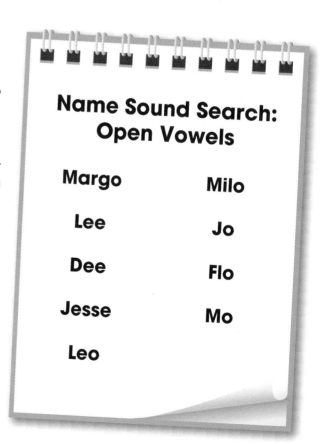

Name Sound Search: Open Vowels

Margo	**Milo**
Lee	**Jo**
Dee	**Flo**
Jesse	**Mo**
Leo	

Name _____

What's the Sound?

Look at each picture. Say the word. Write the ending vowel sound you hear.

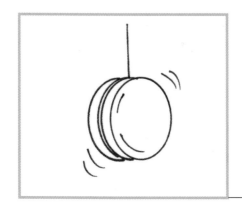

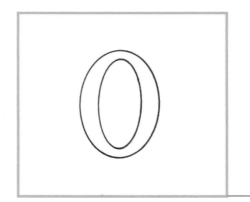

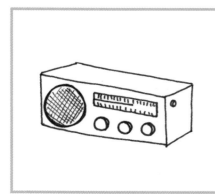

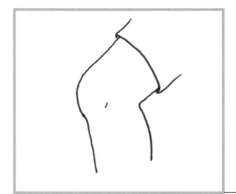

Unit 11 • Everyday Phonics Intervention Activities Grade 2 • ©2010 Newmark Learning, LLC

Name _____

Sort It Out

Cut out each word and read it aloud. Glue the words that end with same sound as _tree_ under the tree. Glue the words that end with the same sound as _rhino_ under the rhino.

go	he	so	be
we	no	Jo	me

Open Vowel Hunt

Find one word in each sentence with an open vowel. Circle the word and write the open vowel on the line.

 I can see. _____

 I go home. _____

 We jump. _____

 He can run. _____

 I say no. _____

Closed Short Vowel to Open Long Vowel

Read the word. Subtract the consonant to make a new word with a long vowel sound. Then read the new word.

got	– t =	
nod	– d =	
sob	– b =	
beg	– g =	
hem	– m =	
met	– t =	
web	– b =	
shed	– d =	

Assessment

Look at the picture pairs. Circle the one with the open vowel. Write the letter that makes the long vowel sound.

Listen to your teacher say each word. Write the words on the lines.

1. _____

2. _____

3. _____

4. _____

5. _____

6. _____

7. _____

Overview   Final Digraph -ck

Directions and Sample Answers for Activity Pages

Day 1	See "Model Final Digraph -ck" below.
Day 2	Read aloud the title and directions. Invite students to name each picture. Then help students identify which words end in **/k/** and color them black. (**chick, smock, truck, clock**)
Day 3	Read aloud the title and directions. Invite students to name each picture clue, explaining that each one ends with the final digraph **-ck**. Then help students complete the crossword by filling in the words. (Across: **3. stick**; **5. jack**; **6. neck**. Down: **1. lock**; **2. lick**; **3. sock**; **4. pack**.)
Day 4	Read aloud the title and directions. Model how to do the first one by reading the word **brim**. Then show how to take away **m** and add **ck** to make the new word **brick**.
Day 5	Read the directions aloud and name the pictures together. Allow time for students to complete the first task. Then pronounce the words **back**, **deck**, **sick**, **mock**, and **tuck** and ask students to write them on the lines. Afterward, meet individually with students to discuss their results. Use their responses to plan further instruction and review.

Model Final Digraph -ck

◆ Hand out the Day 1 activity page and crayons.

◆ **Say:** *Look at the four-leaf clover. It is good luck! Listen for the ending sound as I say the word* **luck** *again:* **/l/ /u/ /k/**. *There is one sound at the end:* **/k/**. *The letters* **c** *and* **k** *together stand for the final* **/k/**.

◆ Ask students to look at the picture of the pond. Write **rock** on the board. **Say:** *Look at the word* **rock**. *Say* **rock** *with me:* **rock**. *Listen as I say it slowly:* **/r/ /o/ /k/**. *Rock ends with a* **/k/** *sound. The letters* **c** *and* **k** *stand for the* **/k/** *sound.*

◆ Help students find and color the other pictures that end with a **c** and **k**. Write the words on the board as you find them: **duck**, **dock**, **shack**, and **kick**. Read each word slowly, pointing out that the **c** and **k** together make a final **/k/** sound.

◆ Point out everyday items that end with a **c** and **k** that make the **/k/** sound. Write a few on chart paper and read the words aloud. Then invite students to add to the list.

**Sound Search:
Final Digraph -ck**

block

brick

clock

lock

Duck Pond

Look at the picture. Color the things that end with a _-ck_ sound.

Unit 12 • Everyday Phonics Intervention Activities Grade 2 • ©2010 Newmark Learning, LLC

Sounds Like Black

Say aloud each picture word. If it ends with the same sound as *black*, color it black.

Name _____

Crossword Puzzle

Say the name of each picture. Then write each picture name in the puzzle.

Across

3

5

6

Down

1    3

2    4

Unit 12 • Everyday Phonics Intervention Activities Grade 2 • ©2010 Newmark Learning, LLC

Name _____

Make a Word

Read the word. Subtract the last letter in the word, add a final *-ck*, and make a new word. Then read the new word.

brim	– m + ck =	
blot	– t + ck =	
crab	– b + ck =	
dug	– g + ck =	
win	– n + ck =	
snag	– g + ck =	
clip	– p + ck =	
trap	– p + ck =	
tug	– g + ck =	
sped	– d + ck =	

Name _____

Assessment

Look at each picture pair. Circle the one with the final digraph *-ck*. Write the letters that make the /k/ sound in that word.

Listen to your teacher say each word. Write the words on the lines.

1. _____

2. _____

3. _____

4. _____

5. _____

Unit 12 • *Everyday Phonics Intervention Activities Grade 2* • ©2010 Newmark Learning, LLC

Overview   Digraphs ch, sh

Directions and Sample Answers for Activity Pages

Day 1	See "Model Digraphs ch, sh" below.
Day 2	Read aloud the title and directions. Invite students to name each picture. Then help students cut out and glue the pictures next to the ones with the same sound in the same position. (sheep: **shoe**. watch: **witch**. brush: **leash**. chick: **cheese**.)
Day 3	Read aloud the title and directions. Invite students to name each picture. Then help students find and write the missing digraph. (**dish, ship, chop, bench**)
Day 4	Read aloud the title and directions. Model how to do the first one by reading the word **mat**. Then show how to take away **m** and add **ch** to make the new word **chat**.
Day 5	Read aloud the directions and name the pictures together. Allow time for students to complete the first task. Then pronounce the words **shed**, **cash**, **chip**, and **such** and ask students to write them on the lines. Afterward, meet individually with students to discuss their results. Use their responses to plan further instruction and review.

Model Digraphs ch, sh

◆ Hand out the Day 1 activity page and crayons.

◆ Write **sh** on the board. Point to the letters as you **say:** *We sit in the shade. Listen for the beginning sound as I say the word **shade** again: **/sh/ /ā/ /d/**. The letters **s** and **h** together make the **/sh/** sound. Listen again for the beginning sound: **/sh/ /ā/ /d/**.*

◆ Write **ch** on the board. Point to the letters as you **say:** *We go to the beach. Listen for the final sound as I say the word **beach** again: **/b/ /ē/ /ch/**. The letters **c** and **h** together make the **/ch/** sound. Listen again for the final sound: **/b/ /ē/ /ch/**.*

◆ Help students find and color the other pictures that begin or end with **/ch/** and **/sh/**. Write the words on the board as you find them and circle the **sh** or **ch**: **fish, shovel, sandwich, children, shell**, and **chair**. Then ask students to draw one more item that begins or ends with **/ch/** or **/sh/**. Invite them to share their drawings with the group.

◆ Point out objects in the classroom that begin or end with **/ch/** or **/sh/**. Write a few on chart paper and read the words aloud. Then invite students to add to the list.

Sound Search: /ch/, /sh/

chalk

chalkboard

shapes

shoe

fish

lunch

children

Shady Beach

Look at the picture. Color the things that have a *ch* or a *sh* sound.

Draw something else that begins or ends with a *ch* or a *sh* sound.

Name _____

Ch or Sh?

Cut out the pictures. Glue each picture in the box that has a picture with /ch/ or /sh/ in the same position.

What's the Word?

Look at each picture. Then write either *ch* or *sh* on the lines to complete the word.

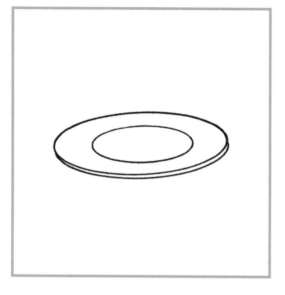

di __ __

__ __ ip

__ __ op

ben __ __

Make a Word

Read the word. Subtract a letter from the beginning or end, and add *ch* or *sh* to make a new word. Then read the new word.

mat	– m + ch =	
rib	– b + ch =	
cop	– c + sh =	
cat	– t + sh =	
pick	– p + ch =	
ink	– k + ch =	
rot	– r + sh =	
lad	– d + sh =	

Assessment

Write _ch_ or _sh_ in front of the picture if it begins with _ch_ or _sh_ and after the picture if it ends with _ch_ or _sh_.

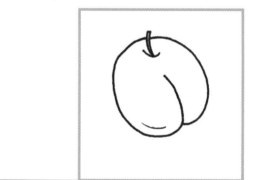

Listen to your teacher say each word. Write the words on the lines.

1. _____

2. _____

3. _____

4. _____

Overview Digraphs th, wh

Directions and Sample Answers for Activity Pages

Day 1	See "Model Digraphs th, wh" below.
Day 2	Read aloud the title and directions. Invite students to name the pictures in each row. Then help students circle the picture that has the same beginning sound as the picture to the left. (wheel: **whale**. thumb: **thermometer**. whistle: **wheat**. thermos: **three**.)
Day 3	Read aloud the title and directions. Invite students to name each picture clue. Then help students identify and write the missing digraph. (**whale, moth, throw, whisk**)
Day 4	Read aloud the title and directions. Model how to do the first one by reading the word **men**. Then show how to take away **m** and add **wh** to make the new word **when**.
Day 5	Read aloud the directions and name the pictures together. Allow time for students to complete the first task. Then pronounce the words **wham**, **thin**, and **math** and ask students to write them on the lines. Afterward, meet individually with students to discuss their results. Use their responses to plan further instruction and review.

Model Digraphs th, wh

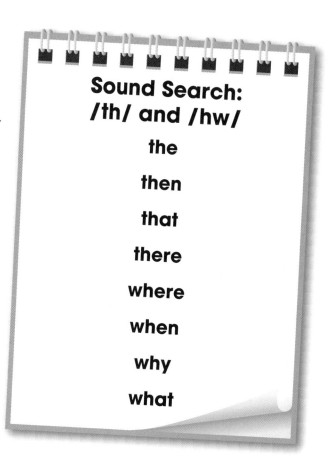

Sound Search:
/th/ and /hw/

the

then

that

there

where

when

why

what

◆ Hand out the Day 1 activity page and crayons.

◆ Write **th** on the board. Point to the letters as you **say:**
Beth is thin. Listen for the final sound as I say the name
Beth *again: /b/ /e/ /th/. The letters t and h together make the /th/ sound. Now listen for the beginning sound in* **thin**: */th/ /i/ /n/. This time the t and h are at the beginning of the word, and again they make the /th/ sound.*

◆ Write **wh** on the board. Point to the letters as you **say:**
What is your name? Listen for the beginning sound as I say the word **what** *again: /hw/ /a/ /t/. The letters w and h together make the /hw/ sound. Now listen again to the beginning sound: /hw/ /a/ /t/.*

◆ Help students find and color the other pictures that begin or end with */th/* and other pictures that begin with */hw/*. Write the words on the board as you find them: **thread**, **cloth**, **thimble**, **wheelchair**, **whiskers**.

◆ Point out words we use all the time that have a */th/* or */hw/* sound. Then invite students to add to the list.

Beth at Home

Look at the picture. Color the things that begin with a *th* or a *wh* sound.

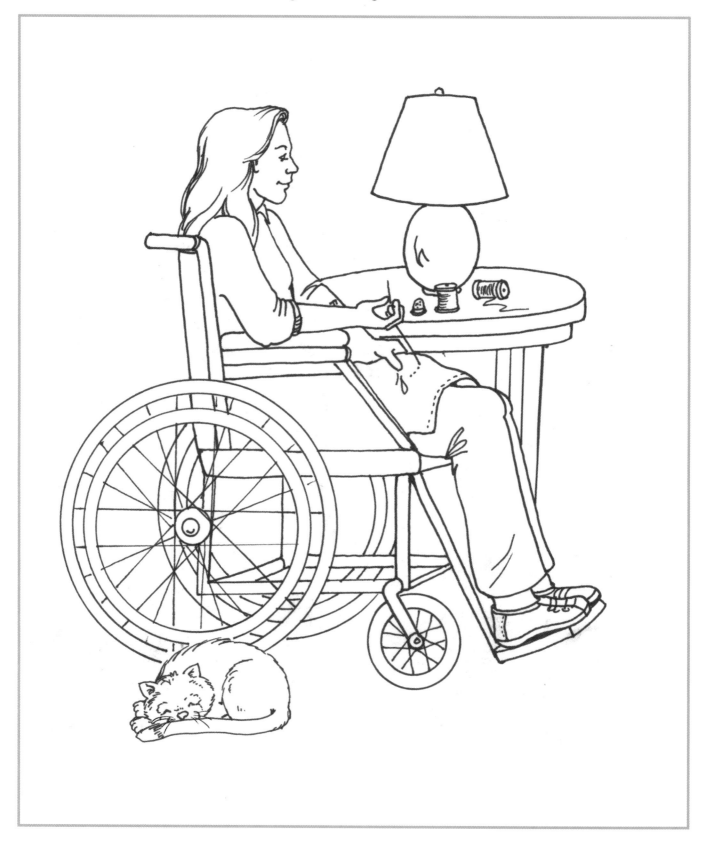

Sounds Like?

In each row, find and circle the picture that has the same beginning sound as the picture on the left.

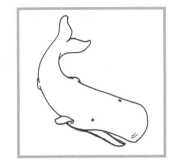

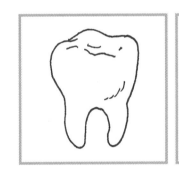
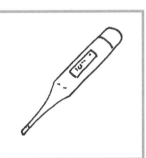

What's the Word?

Look at each picture. Then write either *th* or *wh* on the lines to complete the word.

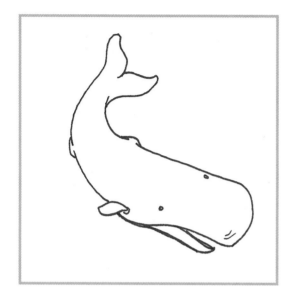

__ __ ale

mo __ __

__ __ row

__ __ isk

Make a Word

Read the word. Subtract a letter from the beginning or end, and add *th* or *wh* to make a new word. Then read the new word.

men	– m + wh =	
bag	– g + th =	
sink	– s + th =	
kite	– k + wh =	
worm	– m + th =	
bank	– b + th =	

Assessment

Write _th_ or _wh_ in front of the picture if it begins with _th_ or _wh_, and write _th_ after the picture if it ends with _th_.

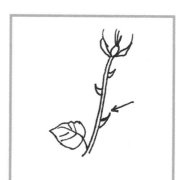

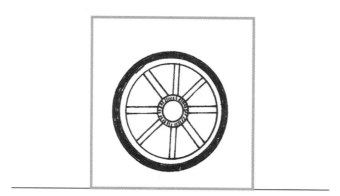

Listen to your teacher say each word. Write the words on the lines.

1. _____

2. _____

3. _____

   Unit 14 • _Everyday Phonics Intervention Activities Grade 2_ • ©2010 Newmark Learning, LLC

Overview   Long a Digraphs

Directions and Sample Answers for Activity Pages

Day 1	See "Model Long a Digraphs" below.
Day 2	Read aloud the title and directions. Invite students to name the pictures. Then help students draw a line from the pictures with the same middle sound as **train** to the train. (**braid, snail, chain, paint**)
Day 3	Read aloud the title and directions. Invite students to name each picture clue. Help them fill in the missing digraphs. Remind them that if the long **a** sound is in the middle, the digraph is **ai**, and if the long **a** is at the end, the digraph is **ay**. (**jail, hay, sail, tray, rain, pay**)
Day 4	Read aloud the title and directions. Model how to do the first one by reading the word **sat**. Point out the short **a** sound. Then show how subtracting the **t** and adding **y** makes the new word **say**. Point out how the letters **ay** create a long **a** sound.
Day 5	Read aloud the directions and name the words together. Allow time for students to complete the first task. Then pronounce the words **laid, rail, pain, saint, wait**, and **bay** and ask students to write them on the lines. Afterward, meet individually with students to discuss their results. Use their responses to plan further instruction and review.

Model Long a Digraphs

◆ Hand out the Day 1 activity page and crayons.

◆ Write **play** and **rain** on the board. Point to the letters as you **say:** *We play in the rain. The words **play** and **rain** both have a long **a** sound. Listen for the end sound as I say the word **play** slowly: /p/ /l/ /ā/. The long **a** sound, or /ā/ comes at the end of the word. The letters **ay** at the end of a word make the long **a** sound.*

◆ **Say:** *Look at the word **rain**. Listen as I say it slowly: /r/ /ā/ /n/. **Rain** has a long **a** sound in the middle of the word. The letters **ai** can stand for the long **a** sound in the middle of words. Color in the rain.*

◆ Help students find and color the other pictures that have the long **a** sound. Write the words on the board as you find them: **mail, tail, Jay**. Read each word slowly, pointing out whether the long **a** comes from **ai** or **ay**.

◆ Point out actions that have a long **a** sound and that have **ai** in the middle or **ay** at the end. Write a few on chart paper and read the words aloud. Then invite students to add to the list.

**Sound Search:
Long a Digraphs**

pay

say

spray

faint

wait

raise

Rainy Day

Look at the picture. Color the things that have a long *a* sound.

Name _____

Picture Match

Draw a line from each picture with the same middle sound as *train.*

What's the Word?

Say the name of the picture and write *ai* or *ay* on the lines to complete the word.

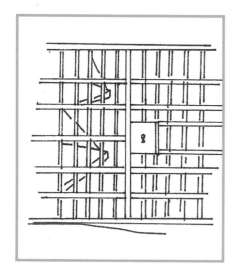

j __ __ l

h __ __

s __ __ l

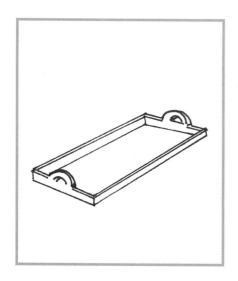

tr __ __

r __ __ n

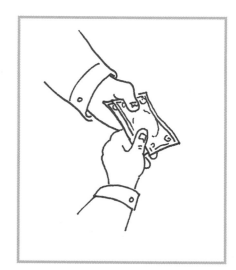

p __ __

Make a Word

Read the word. Subtract a letter and add *ai* or *ay* to make a new word with a long *a* sound. Then read the new word.

sat	– t + y =	
pad	– a + ai =	
man	– a + ai =	
rag	– g + y =	
pal	– a + ai =	
bat	– a + ai =	
clap	– p + y =	
tent	– e + ai =	

Assessment

Read the word pairs. Circle one word in each pair with a long *a* sound. Write the letters that make the /ā/ sound in that word.

pail   pal   _____

mad   maid   _____

day   dad   _____

vain   van   _____

bat   bait   _____

lab   lay   _____

Listen to your teacher say each word. Write the words on the lines.

1. _____   4. _____

2. _____   5. _____

3. _____   6. _____

Overview   Long o Digraphs

Directions and Sample Answers for Activity Pages

Day 1	See "Model Long o Digraphs" below.
Day 2	Read aloud the title and directions. Invite students to name each picture. Then help students circle the picture in each pair that has a long **o** sound. (**blow, goat, toe, cold, hoe, coat, pillow**)
Day 3	Read aloud the title and directions. Invite students to name each picture clue, reminding them that each one includes a long **o** sound. Then help students complete the crossword by filling in the words. (Across: **2. snow**; **3. gold**. Down: **1. goal**; **4. doe**.)
Day 4	Read aloud the title and directions. Model how to do the first one by reading the word **bog**. Point out the short **o** sound. Then show how to subtract the **g** and add **w** to make the new word **bow**. Point out how **ow** creates a long **o** sound.
Day 5	Read aloud the directions and name the pictures together. Allow time for students to complete the first task. Then pronounce the words **soak**, **woe**, **slow**, and **bold** and ask students to write them on the lines. Afterward, meet individually with students to discuss their results. Use their responses to plan further instruction and review.

Model Long o Digraphs

◆ Hand out the Day 1 activity page and crayons.

◆ Write **ow** on the board. Point to the letters as you **say:** *We like the snow. **Snow** has a long **o** sound at the end of the word. The letters **ow** stand for the /ō/ sound.*

◆ Write **oa**, **o**, and **oe** on the board. Point to each in turn as you **say:** *When it snows, you wear a coat because it is cold! If you are not careful, you can freeze your toe. **Coat**, **cold**, and **toe** all have a long **o** sound. Long **o** in the middle of a word is often spelled **oa**, as in **coat**, or **o** if followed by **ld**, as in **cold**. Long **o** at the end of a word, like **toe**, is usually spelled **oe** or **ow**.*

◆ Ask students to look at the picture. **Say:** *Say the word **row** with me: **row**. Listen as I say it again: /r/ /ō/. The **ow** stands for /ō/. Color the oars.*

◆ Repeat with **Joe**, **boat**, **rainbow**, and **gold**.

◆ Point out the names of animals that have a long **o** digraph. List them on chart paper and read the words aloud.

Sound Search: Long o Digraphs

toad   roach

goat   swallow

crow   colt

doe   goldfish

sparrow

Joe Rows a Boat

Look at the picture. Color the things that have a long *o* sound.

Sounds Like Long *o*

Circle the picture in each pair that has a long *o* sound.

 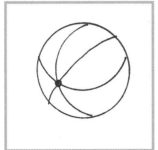  

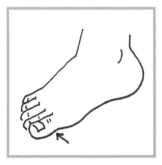   

Crossword Puzzle

Say the name of each picture. Then write each picture name in the puzzle.

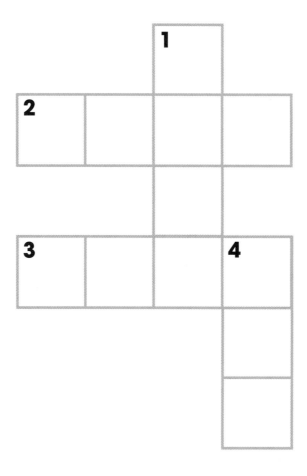

Across

2

3

Down

1

4

Make a Word

Read the word. Subtract a letter and add a new letter or letters to make a new word with a long _o_ sound. Then read the new word.

bog	– g + w =	
fold	– f + g =	
bow	– b + gr =	
moat	– t + n =	
foe	– f + w =	
show	– h + l =	
roam	– m + d =	

Assessment

Read the word pairs. Circle the word in each pair with a long *o* sound. Write the letters that make the long *o* sound in that word.

low   lot   _____

fox   foe   _____

show   shop   _____

cold   cod   _____

Listen to your teacher say each word. Write the words on the lines.

1. _____   3. _____

2. _____   4. _____

Overview   Long e Digraphs

Directions and Sample Answers for Activity Pages

Day 1	See "Model Long e Digraphs" below.
Day 2	Read aloud the title and directions. Invite students to name each picture. Then help students circle the picture in each pair that has a long **e** sound. (**teeth, jeans, wheel, seal, queen, bean**)
Day 3	Read aloud the title and directions. Invite students to read each sentence. Help students circle the word with a long **e** sound and write the letters that stand for the long **e** on the line. (**peas, bee, feed, reads, seed, seat**)
Day 4	Read aloud the title and directions. Model how to do the first one by reading the word **beet**. Then show how to replace the **b** with an **f** to make the new word **feet**. Remind students that **ee** stands for the long **e** sound in **beet** and **feet**.
Day 5	Read aloud the directions and read the word pairs together. Allow time for students to complete the first task. Then pronounce the words **deep**, **meal**, **sheet**, and **steam** and ask students to write them on the lines. Afterward, meet individually with students to discuss their results. Use their responses to plan further instruction and review.

Model Long e Digraphs

◆ Hand out the Day 1 activity page and crayons.

◆ Write **ea** on the board. Point to the letters as you **say:** *There is a leak. Listen for the middle sound as I say the word **leak**: /l/ /ē/ /k/. The letters **ea** stand for the long **e** sound, or /ē/. Listen again for the middle sound: /l/ /ē/ /k/.*

◆ Write **ee** on the board. Point to the letters as you **say:** *She pulled a weed. Listen for the middle sound as I say the word **weed**: /w/ /ē/ /d/. The letters **ee** also stand for the long **e** sound, or /ē/. Listen again for the middle sound: /w/ /ē/ /d/.*

◆ Ask students to look at the picture. **Say:** *Say the word **sweep** with me: **sweep**. Listen as I say it again: /sw/ /ē/ /p/. The **ee** stands for /ē/. Color the woman sweeping.*

◆ Repeat with **cheese, tree, peas, peel, leaves,** and **peach**.

◆ Point out things we do at school that have a long **e** digraph. List them on chart paper and read the words aloud.

Sound Search: Long e Digraph

read	seek
teach	speak
greet	clean
meet	lean
see	eat

Name _____

Green Market

Look at the picture. Color the things that have a long e sound.

Sounds Like Long e

Circle the picture in each pair that has a long *e* sound.

 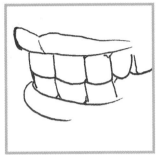

  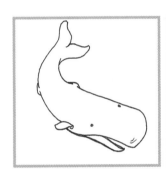 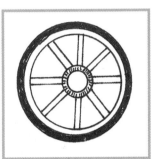

Long e Hunt

Find one word in each sentence that makes a long *e* sound. Circle the word and write the letters that stand for the long *e* sound on the line.

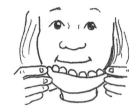 I like peas. _____

 I hit the bee. _____

 Feed the cat. _____

 The boy reads. _____

 The seed is small. _____

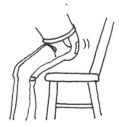 Sit in the seat. _____

Make a Word

Read the word. Subtract a letter or letters and add a new letter or letters to make a new word. Then read the new word.

beet	– b + f =	
seal	– s + r =	
queen	– qu + gr =	
reach	– r + b =	
scream	– sc + d =	
cheek	– ch + cr =	

Assessment

Read the word pairs. Circle the word in each pair with a long *e* sound. Write the letters that make the long *e* sound in that word.

bead   bed   _____

men   mean   _____

pep   peep   _____

check   cheek   _____

Listen to your teacher say each word. Write the words on the lines.

1. _____   3. _____

2. _____   4. _____

Overview Long i Digraphs

Directions and Sample Answers for Activity Pages

Day 1	See "Model Long i Digraphs" below.
Day 2	Read aloud the title and directions. Invite students to name each picture. Then help students circle the picture in each pair that has a long **i** sound. (**tie, eye, knight, rind**)
Day 3	Read aloud the title and directions. Invite students to read each sentence. Help students circle the word with a long **i** sound and write the letters that stand for the long **i** on the line. (**pie, high, bye, wind**)
Day 4	Read aloud the title and directions. Model how to do the first one by reading the word **kind**. Then show how to replace the **k** with an **f** to make the new word **find**. Remind students that **i** sometimes stands for the long **i** sound as in **mind** and **find**.
Day 5	Read aloud the directions and read the word pairs together. Allow time for students to complete the first task. Then pronounce the words **rye**, **bind**, **cried**, and **might** and ask students to write them on the lines. Afterward, meet individually with students to discuss their results. Use their responses to plan further instruction and review.

Model Long i Digraphs

◆ Hand out the Day 1 activity page and crayons.

◆ Write **ie** on the board. Point to the letters as you **say:** *Tie your laces!* **Tie** *has the long* **i** *sound at the end of the word. The letters* **ie** *stand for the* /ī/ *sound.*

◆ Write the words **climb**, **night**, and **bye** on the board. Point to each word in turn as you **say:** *I climb into bed at night and say bye.* **Climb, night,** *and* **bye** *all have the long* **i** *sound.*

◆ Point to **night** and sound out the word by moving your hand under each letter as you say the sound. **Say:** *I see* **i** *followed by* **g** *and* **h**. *The* **igh** *pattern stands for the long* **i** *sound. Watch my finger and listen as I blend this word* /n/ /ī/ /t/. *Repeat with the word* **bye**, *pointing out that the* **ye** *in* **bye** *stands for the long* **i** *sound.*

◆ Ask students to look at the picture. **Say:** *Say the word* **lie** *with me:* **lie**. *Listen as I say it again:* /l/ /ī/. *The* **ie** *stands for* /ī/. *Color the boy lying in the bed.*

◆ Repeat with **light**, **blinds**, and **eye**.

◆ Point out actions that have a long **i** digraph. List them on chart paper and read the words aloud. Invite students to add more to the list.

**Sound Search:
Long i Digraph**

dye

find

tie

fight

Good Night

Look at the picture. Color the things that have a long *i* sound.

Unit 18 • Everyday Phonics Intervention Activities Grade 2 • ©2010 Newmark Learning, LLC

Sounds Like Long i

Circle the picture in each pair that has a long *i* sound.

 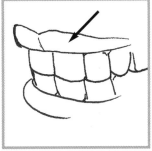

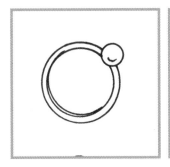 

Long i Hunt

Find one word in each sentence that makes a long *i* sound. Circle the word and write the letters that stand for the long *i* sound on the line.

Pie is good. _____

We go high. _____

He says bye. _____

Wind up the doll. _____

Make a Word

Read the word. Subtract a letter and add a new letter or letters to make a new word with a long *i* sound. Then read the new word.

kind	– k + f =	
mind	– m + gr =	
tie	– t + l =	
sigh	– s + h =	
lye	– l + r =	
flight	– fl + fr =	
skies	– sk + fr =	

Assessment

Read the word pairs. Circle the word in each pair with a long *i* sound. Write the letters that make the long *i* sound in that word.

dries	drip	_____
mind	mean	_____
big	bye	_____
tick	tight	_____
bright	bring	_____
died	did	_____

Listen to your teacher say each word. Write the words on the lines.

1. _____   3. _____

2. _____   4. _____

Overview   y As a Vowel

Directions and Sample Answers for Activity Pages

Day 1	See "Model Examples of y As a Vowel" below.
Day 2	Read aloud the title and directions. Invite students to name the pictures. Then help students cut out the pictures and glue the ones that end in long **e** under the baby and long **i** under the spy. (Baby: **strawberry, twenty, candy.** Spy: **sky, cry, butterfly.**)
Day 3	Read aloud the title and directions. Have students read the sentences. Then help students circle the words that end with the long **i** sound and box the words that end with the long **e** sound. (Long **e**: **rainy, baby, sunny, penny, shiny, puppy, muddy.** Long **i**: **fly, cry, my.**)
Day 4	Read aloud the title and directions. Model how to do the first one by reading the word **me**. Then show how subtracting the **e** and adding **y** makes a new word **my**. Point out how the letter **y** creates a long **i** sound.
Day 5	Read aloud the directions and name the words together. Allow time for students to complete the first task. Then pronounce the words **sly, fry, sixty,** and **dusty** and ask students to write them on the lines. Afterward, meet individually with students to discuss their results. Use their responses to plan further instruction and review.

Model Examples of y As a Vowel

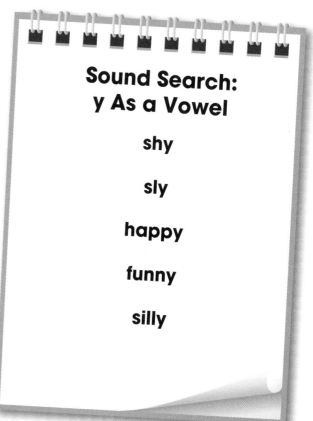

**Sound Search:
y As a Vowel**

shy

sly

happy

funny

silly

◆ Hand out the Day 1 activity page and crayons.

◆ Write **shy** on the board. Point to the letters as you say the word **shy**. **Say:** *Listen for the ending sound as I say the word again: /sh/ /ī/. In the word **shy**, the letter **y** stands for the long i sound.* Point out that the letter **y** is sometimes a vowel, such as in the word **shy**.

◆ Write **happy** on the board. Point to the letters as you say the word **happy**. **Say:** *Listen for the ending sound as I say the word again: /hap/ /ē/. In the word **happy**, the letter **y** stands for the long e sound.* Point out that **happy** ends with the long **e** sound and **shy** ends with the long **i** sound, but both final long vowel sounds are spelled **y**.

◆ Ask students to look at the picture. **Say:** *Say the word **mommy** with me: **mommy**. Listen as I say it again: /mom/ /ē/. The y in mommy stands for /ē/. Color in the mommy.*

◆ Repeat with **baby, cry, daddy,** and **thirsty**. Then ask students to draw one more item that has a **y** as a vowel. Invite them to share their drawings with the group.

◆ Point out that many adjectives, or words we use to describe, have **y** as a vowel. Write a few on chart paper and read the words aloud. Invite students to add to the list.

Cry Baby

Look at the picture. Color the people that have a y as a vowel.

Unit 19 • Everyday Phonics Intervention Activities Grade 2 • ©2010 Newmark Learning, LLC

Sort It Out

Cut out the pictures and say the words aloud. Glue the pictures that end with a long *i* sound under the spy. Glue the pictures that end with a long *e* sound under the baby.

baby

spy

Sounds Like?

Read the sentence. Circle the words that end with a long *i* sound. Put a box around the words that end with a long *e* sound.

 It is a rainy day.

 Get the fly!

 I hear a baby cry.

 It is sunny.

 My penny is shiny.

 The puppy is muddy.

     Unit 19 • Everyday Phonics Intervention Activities Grade 2 • ©2010 Newmark Learning, LLC

Sound Switch-Around

Read the word. Subtract a letter or letters and add a new letter or letters to make a new word. Then read the new word.

me	– e + y =	
cry	– cr + sk =	
fly	– fl + sh =	
spy	– sp + dr =	
funny	– f + s =	
dizzy	– d + f =	
jelly	– j + sm =	
rusty	– r + cr =	
sandy	– s + c =	
lady	– l + sh =	

Name _____

Assessment

Read each word. Check long *i* or long *e* to show the ending vowel sound.

	long **e**	long **i**
fry		
silly		
by		
spy		
kitty		
ninety		

Listen to your teacher say each word. Write the words on the lines.

1. _____

2. _____

3. _____

4. _____

Overview   CVCe Long Vowels Review

Directions and Sample Answers for Activity Pages

Day 1	See "CVCe Long Vowels" below.
Day 2	Read aloud the title and directions. Ask students to cut out the pictures and sort them by vowel sound. (cake: **skate**, **grapes**, **plane**. bike: **slide**, **kite**, **mice**. cone: **globe**, **phone**, **note**.)
Day 3	Read aloud the title and directions. Invite students to name each picture. Then help students unscramble the letters to spell each word.
Day 4	Read aloud the title and directions. Invite students to name each picture. Remind them to listen closely to the middle vowel sound. Then help students fill in the missing letters.
Day 5	Pronounce the following words slowly. Allow time after each word for students to write the word: **take**, **code**, **pine**, **gave**, **joke**, **side**, **ripe**, **same**, **vote**. Afterward, meet individually with students to discuss their results. Use their responses to plan further instruction and review.

CVCe Long Vowels

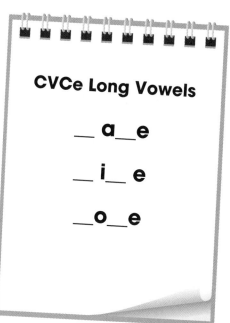

◆ Hand out the Day 1 activity page.

◆ **Say:** *Today we are going to blend words that have a vowel followed by a consonant and a final* **e**. *This pattern tells us that the word has a long vowel sound. We will blend the sounds to read words. Let's look at the first word. Put your finger under the letter* **r** *at the beginning of the word and say the sounds aloud with me, moving your finger as we reach each letter sound.* Model how to blend the sounds. Put your finger under each letter as you extend the sound that each letter stands for. **Say:** **/r/ /ā/ /k/.** Students follow your lead, running their fingers under each letter as you blend them.

◆ **Say:** *What picture shows the word we just read? That's right. We read the word* **rake**. *Now draw a line from the word* **rake** *to the picture of a rake.* Allow students a moment to draw a line connecting the word to the picture.

◆ Have students blend the remaining words by making sure they run their fingers under the letters as they blend the sounds with you. Remind them that the pattern of vowel/consonant/final **e** means that the word has a long vowel sound. Allow time after each word for students to locate and draw a line to the correct picture.

◆ Write the following incomplete words on the board: __ **a__e**; __ **i__ e**; and __**o__e**. Pair students and have them invent a nonsense word for each pattern, such as **zake**, **vife**, and **loje**.

The notepad graphic shows:

CVCe Long Vowels

__ **a__e**

__ **i__ e**

__**o__ e**

Blend, Read, and Match

Read each word. Then draw a line to the matching picture.

rake

kite

rose

tape

pole

cave

dime

bone

dive

Vowel Sound Sort

Cut out the pictures. Sort them in columns by the long vowel sounds.

Word Scramble

Name the pictures. Then unscramble the letters to spell the words.

 oreb   ___ ___ ___ ___

 eimt   ___ ___ ___ ___

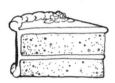 kcea   ___ ___ ___ ___

 evni   ___ ___ ___ ___

 ehlo   ___ ___ ___ ___

 geta   ___ ___ ___ ___

 eopr   ___ ___ ___ ___

 einn   ___ ___ ___ ___

 veaw   ___ ___ ___ ___

Missing Letters

Name the pictures. Listen to the middle vowel sounds. Then write the missing letters on the lines.

h __ m __

p __ p __

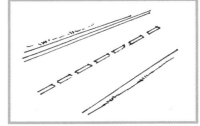

l __ n __

h __ v __

c __ n __

r __ p __

Assessment

Listen to your teacher say each word. Write the words on the lines.

1. _____

2. _____

3. _____

4. _____

5. _____

6. _____

7. _____

8. _____

9. _____

Overview Long Vowel Digraphs Review

Directions and Sample Answers for Activity Pages

Day 1	See "Long Vowel Digraphs" below.
Day 2	Read aloud the title and directions. Invite students to name each picture clue. Tell them that each word has a long **a** sound. Have students complete the crossword. (Across: **3. train**; **4. hay**. Down: **1. braid**; **2. snail**; **3. tray**.)
Day 3	Read aloud the title and directions. Model how to do the first one by reading the word **lie**. Then show how to take away **l** and add **t** to make the new word **tie**.
Day 4	Read aloud the title and directions. Invite students to read the sentences and circle one or more words in each sentence with a long **o** sound. Have them write the letters that make /ō/. (**snow/ow; Joan/oa; goat/oa; toad/oa; row/ow; boat/oa; bow/ow**)
Day 5	Read the directions aloud. Allow time for students to complete the first task. Pronounce the following words slowly. Allow time after each word for students to write the word: **wait, say, tight, fright, slow,** and **road**. Afterward, meet individually with students to discuss their results. Use their responses to plan further instruction and review.

Long Vowel Digraphs

◆ Hand out the Day 1 activity page.

◆ **Say:** *Today you are going to blend words that have long vowel digraphs. You will blend the sounds to read words. Let's look at the first word. Put your finger under the letter **s** at the beginning of the word and say the sounds aloud with me, moving your finger as we reach each letter sound.* Model how to blend the sounds. Put your finger under each letter as you extend the sound that each letter stands for. **Say:** */s/ /ē/ /l/.* Students follow your lead, running their fingers under each letter as you blend them.

◆ **Say:** *What picture shows the word we just read? That's right. We read the word **seal**. Now draw a line from the word **seal** to the picture of a seal.* Allow students a moment to draw a line connecting the word to the picture.

◆ Have students blend the remaining words with long **e** digraphs by making sure they run their fingers under the letters as they blend the sounds with you. Allow time after each word for students to locate and draw a line to the correct picture.

◆ Put ā, ō, ē, and ī on index cards in a pocket chart. Distribute words on index cards with the different long vowel digraphs, including **high, pie, bean, green, show, load, bay,** and **gain**. Ask students to read the words and place them under the correct long vowel.

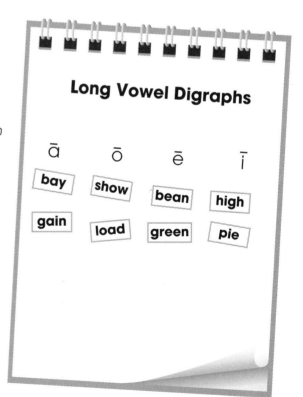

Long Vowel Digraphs

ā	ō	ē	ī
bay	show	bean	high
gain	load	green	pie

Blend, Read, and Match

Read each word. Then draw a line to the matching picture.

seal

pea

wheel

tea

beak

bee

meat

three

Name _____

Long *a* Crossword Puzzle

Say the name of each picture. Then write each picture name in the puzzle.

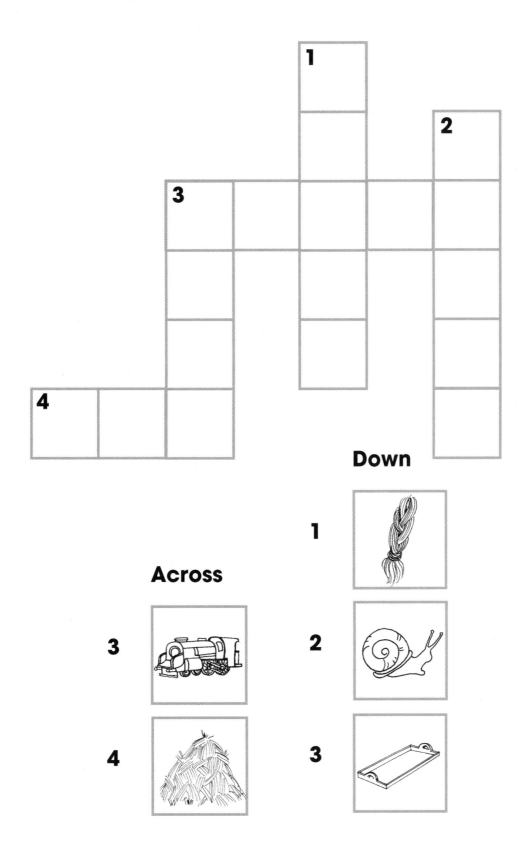

Down

1

Across

3

4

2

3

Make a Word

Read the word. Subtract a letter or letters and add a new letter or letters to make a new word with a long *i* sound. Then read the new word.

lie	– l + t =	
fight	– f + r =	
cried	– cr + fr =	
thigh	– th + s =	
might	– m + n =	
flies	– fl + sp=	

Unit 21 • Everyday Phonics Intervention Activities Grade 2 • ©2010 Newmark Learning, LLC

Long *o* Hunt

Find one or more words in each sentence that makes a long *o* sound. Circle the words and write the letters that stand for the long *o* sound on the lines.

I love snow.

_____

Joan has a goat.

_____

I see a toad!

_____

Row the boat.

_____

Her bow is big.

_____

Assessment

Match words in the columns that have the same long vowel sound.

wait	heel
bean	bye
low	pay
high	soak

Listen to your teacher say each word. Write the words on the lines.

1. _____   4. _____

2. _____   5. _____

3. _____   6. _____

Overview Initial Blends Review

Directions and Sample Answers for Activity Pages

Day 1	See "Initial Blends" below.
Day 2	Read aloud the title and directions. Have students cut out each picture and paste it under the picture that begins with the same blend. (**skis/skates; frog/fruit; snake/snail; slide/sled; broom/bridge; cloud/clock**)
Day 3	Read aloud the title and directions. Have students write the blends to make rhyming words. Then have them draw what they wrote. (**flag, frog, swing, skip**)
Day 4	Read aloud the title and directions. Invite students to name each picture. Then have them fill in the missing letters.
Day 5	Pronounce the following words slowly. Allow time after each word for students to write the word: **blot, clay, flip, glad, plan, slab, skin, smog, snip, span, stop, swam, brat, crop, drip, from, grin,** and **prop**. Afterward, meet individually with students to discuss their results. Use their responses to plan further instruction and review.

Initial Blends

◆ Hand out the Day 1 activity page.

◆ Write the words **clap, drab, snap** in a row on the board. Point out that each word starts with a different type of blend. Remind students that a blend is two or three letters that stand for a blended sound. Circle each blend as you read it and tell students what blend family each belongs to (**l**-family, **r**-family, or **s**-family).

◆ Point to the word **flag** at the top of the activity page. Model sounding out the word, blending each sound as you run your finger under the letters: **/fl/ /a/ /g/**. Then say the whole word. Point out that the words starts with an **l**-family blend.

◆ **Say:** *What picture shows the word we just read? That's right. We read the word* **flag***. Now draw a line from the word* **flag** *to the picture of a flag.* Allow students a moment to draw a line connecting the word to the picture.

◆ Have students blend the remaining words. Allow time after each word for students to locate and draw a line to the correct picture.

◆ Write the following incomplete words on the board: **fl__ __; sn__ __; br__ __; pl__ __; st__ __; gr__ __.** Pair students and have them build a word starting with each blend.

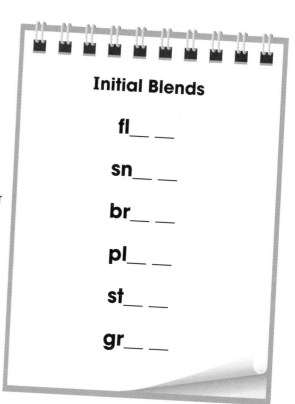

Initial Blends

fl__ __

sn__ __

br__ __

pl__ __

st__ __

gr__ __

Blend, Read, and Match

Read each word. Then draw a line to the matching picture.

flag

swan

crab

plane

star

drum

Sound Match

Cut out each picture and paste it under the picture that begins with the same blend.

Rhyming Words

Review the blends at the bottom. Write the blends to make rhyming words. Then draw a picture of each word.

hag

___ ag

log

___ ___ og

ring

___ ___ ing

rip

___ ___ ip

| sw | fl | sk | fr |

Unit 22 • Everyday Phonics Intervention Activities Grade 2 • ©2010 Newmark Learning, LLC

Missing Letters

Name the pictures. Listen to the initial blend sounds. Then write the missing letters on the lines.

___ ___ ib

___ ___ ow

___ ___ ate

___ ___ ant

___ ___ ir

___ ___ ow

___ ___ ot

___ ___ ush

Name _____

Assessment

Listen to your teacher say each word. Write the words on the lines.

1. _____

2. _____

3. _____

4. _____

5. _____

6. _____

7. _____

8. _____

9. _____

10. _____

11. _____

12. _____

13. _____

14. _____

15. _____

16. _____

17. _____

18. _____

UNIT 23

Overview   Final Blends Review

Directions and Sample Answers for Activity Pages

Day 1	See "Final Blends" below.
Day 2	Read aloud the title and directions. Have students cut out each picture and paste it under the picture that ends with the same blend. (**cast/vest; wink/link; wand/pond; tent/paint; stump/jump**)
Day 3	Read aloud the title and directions. Model how to do the first one by reading the word **rest**. Then show how to take away **r** and add **b** to make the new word **best**.
Day 4	Read aloud the title and directions. Invite students to name each picture. Then have them fill in the missing letters.
Day 5	Pronounce the following words slowly. Allow time after each word for students to write the word: **left**, **gulp**, **tilt**, **bump**, **stink**, **want**, and **dust**. Afterward, meet individually with students to discuss their results. Use their responses to plan further instruction and review.

Final Blends

◆ Hand out the Day 1 activity page.

◆ Write the words **bent**, **clunk**, **fond**, **jump**, **lift**, **felt**, **help**, and **past** in a row on the board. Point out that each word ends with a different type of blend. Remind students that a blend is two or three letters that stand for a blended sound. Circle each final blend as you read it and tell students what blend family each word belongs to (**nt, nk, nd, mp, ft, lt, lp,** or **st**).

◆ Point to the word **belt** at the top of the activity page. Model sounding out the word, blending each sound as you run your finger under the letters: **/b/ /e/ /l/ /t/**. Then say the whole word. Point out that the word ends with a two-letter blend.

◆ **Say:** *What picture shows the word we just read? That's right. We read the word **belt**. Now draw a line from the word **belt** to the picture of a belt.* Allow students a moment to draw a line connecting the word to the picture.

◆ Have students blend the remaining words. Allow time after each word for students to locate and draw a line to the correct picture.

◆ Write the following final two-letter blends on the board with lines preceding them: __ __ **ft**; __ __**lp**; __ __ **lt**; __ __ **mp**; __ __ **nd**; __ __ **nk**; __ __ **nt**; __ __ **st**. Pair students and have them build a word ending with each blend.

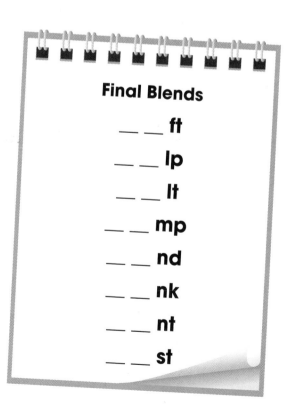

Final Blends

__ __ **ft**

__ __ **lp**

__ __ **lt**

__ __ **mp**

__ __ **nd**

__ __ **nk**

__ __ **nt**

__ __ **st**

Blend, Read, and Match

Read each word. Then draw a line to the matching picture.

belt

stamp

gift

hand

skunk

ant

nest

Sound Match

Cut out each picture and paste it under the picture that ends with the same blend.

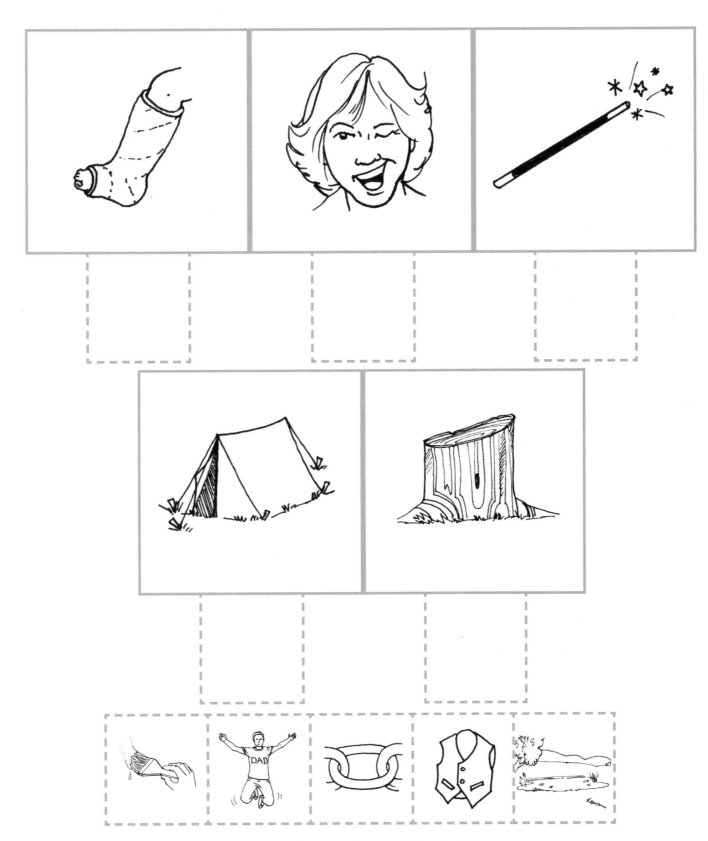

Blend Math

Solve each word equation and write the new words on the lines.

rest	– r + b =	
bent	– b + r =	
lump	– l + p =	
craft	– cr + dr =	
help	– h + y =	
felt	– f + m =	
mink	– m + p =	
grand	– gr + st =	

Unit 23 • Everyday Phonics Intervention Activities Grade 2 • ©2010 Newmark Learning, LLC

Missing Letters

Name the pictures. Listen to the final blend sounds. Then write the missing blends on the lines.

 li ___ ___

 sa ___ ___

  chi ___ ___

 ha ___ ___

 si ___ ___

 de ___ ___

 ne ___ ___

Name _____

Assessment

Listen to your teacher say each word. Write the words on the lines.

1. _____

2. _____

3. _____

4. _____

5. _____

6. _____

7. _____

 Unit 23 • Everyday Phonics Intervention Activities Grade 2 • ©2010 Newmark Learning, LLC